A Gathering of Cranes
Bringing the Tao to the West

Solala Towler

Abode of the Eternal Tao
Eugene, Oregon

ii

Published by
The Abode of the Eternal Tao
4852 West Amazon
Eugene, OR 97405

Printed in the United States of America

ISBN 0-9649912-0-9

Dedicated to the memory of my first Taoist teacher, David Cheng.

Foreword

In China, cranes have long been a symbol of wisdom and longevity. Expressions like 'heavenly crane' *(tian-he)* or 'blessed crane' *(xian-he)* describe the role of the crane as a symbol of wisdom. The death of a Taoist priest is called *yu-hua* or 'turning into a feathered (crane)'.

The animals themselves are non-aggressive and quiet in nature. Living in harmony with each other, they are brave in the face of danger and never yield to violence.

It is in this spirit that the nine teachers interviewed in this book are presented. Each teacher, in their own unique way, exemplifies these attributes of wisdom, gentleness, and openness. Each one, though originally from the East, has chosen to make their home in and their teachings available to the West. In this way, they are creating a new approach which blends the wisdom and harmony of the East with the forthrightness and open-mindedness of the West.

It is this blending, this sharing from the heart, this new child of Eastern and Western parents, that this book is all about. The wisdom and teachings presented here are often extremely ancient yet completely up-to-date. They are as useful for today's problems as they were for those of ancient China and do not demand any religious conversion to utilize them.

In publishing *The Empty Vessel*, I have had the good fortune to meet with many teachers, both Chinese and American. The wisdom and joy they have shared with me has given me the inspiration to produce this volume. Here, we are showcasing nine national-level teachers, all originally from China, who have decided to bring the wisdom of the ancient achieved ones to the West.

Join us then for this gathering of cranes, this sharing from the heart of nine teachers, each in their own way an example of what Chuang Tzu meant when he described the sage as "one who has a free mind, a calm manner, and an unfurrowed brow; is as cool as autumn and as mild as spring; is in harmony with all things and has no limitations."

Contents

Acknowledgments

First I would like to thank the nine teachers included in this book who gave of their time and their insights. Without them and their generosity in sitting for these interviews, this book would not have been possible.

I would also like to thank C.R. Harper for her help in editing and proofreading, a demanding and often tedious job but one which is, nonetheless, vital to any book.

And, lastly, I would like to thank my wife Christine for her support and encouragement, which made the whole thing possible.

Introduction

Carrying Taoism to the West

In using the term Taoism, I refer to that philosophy of ancient China which gave birth to what we today know as Traditional Chinese Medicine, the practices of *tai ji* and *qi gong*, as well as books of self-cultivation such as the *I Ching* and the *Tao Te Ching*. This tradition goes back thousands of years, to a time before organized religion, before ideologies overcame philosophy. It goes back to a time when humankind was not disconnected from the natural world, when humans learned from both the animal and the vegetable kingdom.

By watching very closely what animals did when they were sick or injured, early Taoist herbalists learned which herbs could be used for sickness or injury to humans. By ingesting various combinations of plants and minerals, they were able to discern which combinations were helpful for a myriad of human ills. In deep meditation they were able to track how energy or *qi* moves in the human body and thereby discover the meridians or channels and the points of intersection that acupuncturists use today. Also, by watching how animals move and even how they compose themselves for rest, these ancient natural scientists were able to develop moving exercises or forms (today called *qi gong*) that were able to facilitate energy movement and healing in the human body.

True Taoism is not an ideology or a new age movement, it is a living philosophy. It is a way of thinking, a way of looking at life, a way of being; being *with* change rather than against it. It is a way of utilizing the natural energy of our bodies and minds in a healthy and graceful way.

Around 2500 years ago Lao Tzu, in response to the moral and physical decay of his time, wrote a short, simple treatise on self-cultivation that today we call the *Tao Te Ching*. Perhaps our present society mirrors his. Everywhere we look today we see signs of turbulence and turmoil: racism, violence, despair and a health care system based on technology that puts the spirit of the patient last. Is it any wonder that people are searching for something to fill the vast emptiness they feel inside?

The pure philosophy of Tao with its emphasis on self-cultivation and self-responsibility and its many forms of energy work and exercise are perfect for today's world. Taoism is not a foreign, ancient, or mystical path. It is as useful for today's problems and interests as those of the Tang dynasty!

Yet, our Western culture is very different from that of the Chinese. Our lifestyle and our environment are different. While the actual practice of *qi gong* and *tai ji* is universal, we in the West approach our practices in a different way than people do in China.

For instance: Westerners do not always learn best by rote memorization, the dedication to get up at five in the morning to practice is not prevalent, and the patience to stick with a practice for years at a time before noticing major changes is rare. Since we have religious freedom in the West, people are free to pick and choose in the spiritual supermarket, one day dabbling in *tai ji*, the next in Zen and the next in flying saucers, or perhaps all of the above at once!

What we in the West need to learn is how to focus; deeply and intentionally. Only then will we begin to make progress on our spiritual path. We must learn the joys of a long and sustained practice and what a difference in our lives it can make.

The idea that we need to become pseudo-Asians to make use of the teachings of Tao is wrong. The important thing is that we must be true to ourselves, to our own culture, our own history, our own unique place in the world.

Qi gong, like music, is a universal language. The place we in the West arrive at in our practice is the very same place that Chinese practitioners arrive at. There is really no need to travel to far-off lands to study the Tao. It is certainly interesting to explore and experience how other people live and practice, but we can do the most good for ourselves by creating and sustaining our own practice wherever we are. Remember, Lao Tzu said:

Without going outside, you may know the whole world.
Without looking through the window, you may see the ways of heaven.
The further you go, the less you know.

Taoism is a belief in life, a belief in the glorious procession of each unfolding moment. It is a deeply spiritual way of life, involving introspection, balance, emotional and spiritual independence and responsibility. It also involves a deep awareness of and connection to the earth and all other life forms, an understanding of how energy works in the body and how to treat illness in a safe, non-invasive manner.

A Taoist is someone who believes in the divinity, specialness and deep down holiness of each individual, including themselves. As Hua Ching Ni tells us, "An undistorted human life is the real model of all universal truth." The Taoist seeks to dig down deep under all the layers of cultural and psychological silt that have accumulated in humans over the millennia and bring forth the shining pearl that lies beneath.

Just like Bodhidarma is said to have carried Buddhism to China, so too has Taoism been carried to the West on the backs of teachers like the ones in this book. It is up to us now, as students of Tao, to take the next important steps in planting the seeds of Tao in our own land. Then, with our dedication and work, we will be able to watch those seeds sprout and grow into great beautiful forests.

Solala Towler, editor

Glossary

Note: I have decided to put this simple glossary in the beginning of the book, rather than at the end, so that my readers may be better able to familiarize themselves with the most common Taoist terms used by the teachers in this book before they begin reading. Chinese terms are spelled in the modern *pinyin* style, except for a few words like Taoism, in order to avoid confusion.

Qi. (Chee) Basic life force, the energy that motivates and sustains the universe and us in it.

Qi Gong. (Chee Gong) Working with *qi*. Usually a series of exercises including movements or postures accompanied by visualizations.

Tai Ji Quan. A form of *qi gong*. Usually a form or series of graceful slow movements to stimulate the flow of *qi* in the body.

Jing. The first of the Three Treasures (along with *shen* and *qi*). Prenatal *qi*, which we inherit from our parents at conception, governs constitution and regulates the hormonal and reproductive systems. It is sometimes called essence and is stored in the kidneys.

Shen. Spirit, consciousness. Resides in the heart and rules what the Chinese consider the mind.

Hsein. (Shen) An immortal or realized being.

Feng Shui. (Fung Shway) Literally wind and water. A system of geomancy which considers the relationship between the individual or building and its environment.

Yin/Yang. The two primal polarities of energy in the universe. Can also symbolize man/woman, light/dark, inside/outside etc.

Dan Tien: The three major energy centers of the body, including upper (third eye), middle (solar plexus), and lower (lower abdomen).

1
Morality Is The
Mother of Qi Gong

Hui Xian Chen

Hui Xian Chen, or Professor Chen, as she likes to be called, is a lively, lovely woman in her sixties who radiates health and vitality. She has literally changed her life and healed herself from a serious cancer with the practice of *qi gong*, because of this, she feels that she has a mission to impart that knowledge to the West. The fact that she was a professor of English for many years in Beijing makes it possible for her to communicate easily with Westerners. Like many people from modern China, she did not grow up in a Taoist tradition, but since then has developed a deep understanding of the spiritual roots of *qi gong*. She has a warm and caring concern for her students and is ready at any moment with a helping hand, a funny story or an inspiring tale. For those who know her, to speak with her and, especially, to study with her, is an honor and a privilege. She lives in Portland, Oregon and teaches at the Oregon School of Oriental Medicine.

You have an interesting story about how you got involved with qi **gong** ***don't you?***

That's right. Right now, when you look at me, do I look healthy?

You look fine to me.

Yes, but actually ever since I was young I was always sick. Then when I was at the University I had trouble with arthritis. Sometimes I could not stand up to answer my teacher's questions. In China, when the students are asked to answer a question they stand up, to show respect for the teacher. I couldn't stand up! Things like that.

Did you work with traditional Chinese doctors then?

At that time, but not much. We had a school clinic. We were poor students, so the only thing we could do was to go to the school clinic. They gave me pills, which didn't really help. I graduated from the University at the age of twenty, and often felt ill; very often. In general, my personality is very active. I liked to go out to meet people, but physically I was weak.

Later I got married at the age of twenty four, but that marriage was not a happy one, so I was more depressed and my health deteriorated. Then came the Cultural Revolution.

Were you a teacher then?

Yes, I was an interpreter for the Minister of the Foreign Trade for six years. After that, I became a teacher of English at the University up until I retired two years ago. All that time I was so sick, especially after the Cultural Revolution, because I was sent to the country and brainwashed to change my so-called bourgeoisie ideas and all that.

Finally, I was allowed to come back and teach in a coastal city, Da Lian, where I taught for about twelve years. That period of time was really the hardest. It was there that I developed a cancer which was very serious. I did not find out until I went to Beijing and went to a doctor who told me I had breast cancer. It was one of the most dangerous kind. I was taken to the hospital and operated on. Then, I had chemotherapy and radiation treatment, which helped, but I couldn't really stand it. I was very, very weak with on-going headaches. By then, the cancer had spread through my lymph system. Everyone thought I was dying.

Finally I left the hospital, but came back for my chemotherapy and radiation treatments. I was still too weak to stand it. At that time, I met a fellow patient in the clinic who told me that I should try *qi gong*. He had come from another province and was refused admittance at the hospital because he was considered a hopeless case. He had very advanced lung cancer.

He didn't want to just leave Beijing without anything. So he stayed there in a hotel and began looking for some kind of secret prescription. In the morning he would try to go out and walk and saw people doing something very strange in the park. He went up to them and asked them what it was they were doing, and they said "We are practicing *qi gong*." He had never heard of this. Then the people there began to tell him about their own stories and he began practicing with them. He was taught a type of *qi gong* called Soaring Crane *Qi Gong*.

This is the style that I later learned and that I now teach. I also know other types of *qi gong*, but basically I teach this style.

Anyway, my fellow patient began to practice this *qi gong* and after one month he said he could feel his body changing. He felt much, much better. Then, after two months of practicing, he went back to the doctor and asked to be examined again. To the doctors' great surprise, only one cancer was left, so that they decided that they could do radiation on that one. So that is what he was doing there.

He helped me to register and get into the workshop. Then he left Beijing once he was well and I never saw him again. I am very thankful to him. So I started practicing in the winter of 1982. It was very hard. I lived very far from the park where we practiced. I had to walk for a half an hour just to get to the bus station to take me into town. Every morning at four o'clock I had to get up and walk very slowly to the bus station, then I took a bus to the park. My teacher was a student of the master of this style of *qi gong*. He was always there waiting in the snow for the students. Then we would begin practice at six o'clock in the morning out in the cold winds of Beijing. Very hard!

I learned the Soaring Crane style of *qi gong*. There are five routines to start with. We learned very slowly because we were all so sick. After three weeks, practicing three hours a day, I already felt much better. My appetite came back. I felt like going out to see a movie! I began to look at the world differently. I came to life again and became happier day by day.

I was staying with a relative then, and my nephew, who was only eleven years old at the time, helped me a lot. Every day he would accompany me to the park and take care of me. I learned the basic five routines and the standing meditation. Later on I learned much more, the more advanced techniques, but in the beginning those basic routines gave me my health back.

So, after three months I felt very different. People would look at me and say "Wow, you look like you've come back to life again!" My hair began to grow back.

Was this form originated by Zhao Jin-Xiang, or is it an old form?

He originated it. Although he once told me that it was not actually his invention. It was a message that he got. When he was sixteen years old he was very sick with tuberculosis and weighed only 90 pounds. He was sent to a sanitorium where he learned a traditional seated meditation. Then he began learning Chinese medicine through books. He learned how to prescribe for other people. He was then able to cure himself.

He went back to his hometown to visit his parents. On the train he met a peasant farmer-type of man seated across from him who was staring at him. When Master Zhao asked him why he was staring at him the man said, "I know you practice *qi gong*." Master Zhao said, "No no, I do not practice." But the man said that Master Zhao was gifted in *qi gong* and that he would teach him. So the man told him to hold the corner of his coat. When Master Zhao started to touch his coat the man said. "No, I mean to hold it with your mind. I am going to take you on a journey."

Immediately Master Zhao felt like he was floating in the sky and looking down at the train. He was very scared but eventually his energy came back to his body. The man never did tell him his name but just told him to study hard and said some day he would teach. He then told him to visit some of the Taoists in the mountains, which later Master Zhao did.

After that Master Zhao came back to Beijing. The word got out that he would help cure people. The problem was, that so many people came to him to be treated that he was surrounded by people. So he decided to develop a type of *qi gong* that would be helpful to all people. The problem was, he had had only four years of schooling, and it was not easy for him to draw. Then, one night in a dream, he was taught all the five routines. He was told to go out and teach people. This was at the end of the Cultural Revolution, so people were starting to do *tai ji* practice in the park or just doing walking exercise. So he went to the park and met eight people who were very very ill with fatal diseases with an average age of sixty or more. These were ready to catch a straw! So they were ready to try. They had to hide themselves in the woods so that they would not be hassled by the guards in the park, since things were very hard at that time.

After three months, all of them became cured and were allowed to go back to work. The word spread like mushrooms after a rain. So Master Zhao sent out eight people to teach other people. After about five years about eleven million people were practicing this type of *qi gong.* Today there are around twenty million people practicing. So he was a pioneer.

Do you think there is much respect or attention to spiritual matters in China today? Years ago there was not much emphasis on that.

That is true. Even myself, when I first began to practice *qi gong* it was because I wanted to get my health back. The way I was raised, being educated in Marxism, Leninism and Mao Tse Tung thought, we didn't believe in the spiritual side of things. But now it is coming back.

When I teach, I bring out the spiritual side of *qi gong* right away. I don't want to hide it. In the old days the masters had to be very careful about teaching that type of thing. After you reached a certain level, then they would teach you. I began to have a type of out of body experience after practicing for years. I asked, "What was that?" My soul went out to visit other places. So I went back to ask my master what did that mean? I didn't understand. Then he began to explain to me that these were called out-of body experiences. He said that I had been given a taste of the spiritual world.

My purpose right now is to train more teachers so that they can go out and teach. *Qi gong* will definitely benefit the people. In the first place, it affects the body, the physical body. Then very quickly you will find it will affect your spiritual self. I think of it as the very first step in a long journey. It's a gift from the universe. The world is changing right now, the vibrational frequency is changing. If people do not practice and adjust themselves to the changing environment they will not be able to adapt to the changes. There will be many spiritual changes, also, and the change of the mind is the number one important thing for this work. The law of nature is Tao, and *qi gong* brings people to the Tao. There are many types of *qi gong* as well as many other types of spiritual practice. The U.S. is open to everything, which is very good.

Many people in this country are studying qi gong now; learning the forms, the practice, and the techniques. Yet a lot of teachers don't talk to their students about the spiritual side, or what you call the morality side, of qi gong.

The major purpose of *qi gong* is to bring people to a higher state of consciousness. We say that the highest level of *qi gong* is to pursue Tao, but you must pursue Tao from everyday life. Whatever you say, whatever you think, all your actions, should be on the right path. In order to guide people onto the right path, to pursue Tao, you have to get people started. You need to have a way to help them. Different religions and different spiritual teachers do this in their own way.

According to my experience, *qi* itself is medicine. It is also consciousness. In China, at that time, I could not talk about the spiritual aspect, but many things happened to me, just through the practice. I was not taught, I was never told about the spiritual aspect of *qi gong*. I was sick and so I just wanted to catch the last straw! I had many experiences. One time, all of a sudden, I felt that I did not exist. My body disappeared and only the consciousness existed there. It only lasted for one or two minutes. I felt that "Ah, this is nothingness!"

I feel that actually, when you reach that stuff, then you really know the source of the universe. So everything will go back to that void, nothingness. You just feel consciousness, you are conscious of everything but the body is dissolved. Sometimes I felt that my head was disappearing. Oh, there's no head, so light. Or sometimes I felt like one arm was missing or one leg or part of me was missing. It was very strange.

Of course, now, I don't encourage people to have out of body experiences or to have visions. I now understand. In the beginning I was very much attracted by those spiritual powers. Now I understand that spiritual powers are the powers you get on your spiritual path. What I learned from my own spiritual powers is that there are other worlds. There are other levels in the universe. I was brought up in a society that taught that apart from this planet, there is nothing. I did not really believe that there are other life forms on other planets or in the spirit world. Soon my experiences, and vision or the fact that I could communicate with other life forms changed my mind. Now I understand that all those experiences were given to me to teach me to be aware of the truth of the universe. I had my eyes wide open and I saw things. I saw the light in the people passing by. I could see the upper *dan tien*, the middle *dan tien* and the lower *dan tien*. I could see a thick column of light coming out from their head, how high it was. I could see the light coming out from different plants, from trees, flowers. I could see many things through my third eye, all of which taught me a lot.

Why do you now discourage students from those kinds of experiences?

All these are lower level things. At that time, I was very impressed and thought it was great! I went to Master Zhao and he looked at me very sternly. I told him that I could see his aura around him very clearly. He said to me "Oh, you have very good eyes. I have heard that you have many powers. Tell me about them." So I began to tell him about them. He told me to stop. He said if you do them you are either going to reduce your power or you will add to your age. "What's the problem?" I asked. I thought I was doing good, helping to publicize Soaring Crane *qi gong* and here he was yelling at me! I did not understand. I said, "You are not happy that your student has this kind of power?"

Then later I had another chance to talk with him. He said for me to tell him all my stories. I started to tell him what I saw, where I went and so on. I asked him what it was all about. He told me that I had been given only a taste of the spiritual world. I still didn't understand because I thought that there was no spiritual world.

Because of the way you were raised?

Yes. Because I was raised in that way. Then he said something like "You've been in the sea of bitterness so long that it is time for you to come ashore". I thought to myself, "Wow, my master is so superstitious." He sounded like some sort of monk. I did not know at the time that he was a Buddhist. Then he started to tell me that I was to forget about all my powers and focus on Tao. I did not know what he meant by "Tao". It was too vague. I thought I was great. I had all kinds of spiritual powers and liked showing off. I was interested in anyone with psychic powers.

Then later on, we were teaching cosmic language and all the students could do it but me. I was laughing and happy when they were doing it. Then later on I told Master Zhao that it seemed like now I had nothing left. He said, "Are you asking for that?" I said that here I was the teacher and my students were higher than me! He said, "No you have passed that stage. Your mission is to pursue Tao". I remember very clearly. So in that way he really encouraged me. He also didn't want me to heal people. I had a lot of healing powers but he didn't want me to heal people. He said that my mission was to be a teacher.

As far as the morality part of it—when I first began learning *qi gong* the teacher said no morality, no *qi gong*. In *qi gong* you get positive energy from the universe to help you. If you don't have morality you will get negative *qi*. If you are morally right, we say that right thinking brings about right energy. The wrong thinking brings you the negative energy. There are two different kinds of energy. It all depends on your thought, on your mind. So it is important to have the right motivation, the right thinking all the time.

Whatever goes round, comes round. I do not know my past life, I do not know my future, but I can see what has been happening to me. I see what has been happening to the people around me; what they did when they were younger, and now that they are old, what has happened to them. And I already see the karma. If you do not treat people well, they do not treat you well. It comes back to you. This is the law of the universe.

If you are morally wrong you cannot do the right thing. If you are morally high, you always help people. For instance, if I treat Solala well then he will smile at me. When he sees me he will say "Hi Chen!" I will say "Solala!" and then we will give each other a big hug. It's very natural. If I have not done good to you when you see me you will turn around and try to avoid my sight, right? Or even when we don't meet each other and you are at home, when you think of me you will think, "Eh, Chen is really no good!" Right?

So, however you send out the messages, whatever you think, it works. Thinking is very important. So we say that if we want to change this world we have to change the mind. The way of thinking is very important. When you think negatively you send out the negative energy to the person you are thinking of. When you think positively you are sending positive energy. It is true. This energy just goes.

If you are morally right; you love people, you share with people, you are forgiving, kind, and helpful, and people react in a good way. Energy-wise you get a lot of good energy. You're happy. To me, to practice *qi gong*, to do meditation—the finer purpose is to help yourself become happy, to make people around you happy, to make the whole world happy, to bring peace to this world. At the same time, you pave the way for yourself after death, because the soul will exist in the universe forever. This is the everlasting part of our selves. The *qi* or the breath will go away when the body dies. When *yin* and *yang* are not balanced they split and then the genuine *qi*, the spirit, goes away. Where does it go? It must go somewhere. Now I know.

We say birds of a feather flock together. If your spiritual consciousness is high, very naturally the planet with a very high frequency will attract the high level spirits. If morally you are not good, even if you do the routines very well, it doesn't mean anything. Then the soul will be attracted to the lower energy forms where you will find people at your level. It may be very low. People there will fight with you and hate you. It's hell. To me hell is not really someplace where people just saw you in half and so on. There are places even in this society where we have different levels. As spiritual people, we are happy together, but in some communities people only talk about money or family things or how to rape people, how to rob them, how to kill people. They're in hell. They are not happy. We are happy because spiritually we are high. So after death the spiritual part exits and goes to where it belongs. It is the law of nature.

So to me, to do meditation is not just to sit there and be blank. I think a lot. It is important to think, because the mind is for thinking. Either you think of money, you think of doing things, you think of work, think of shopping, or marrying and so on. Why not think of the big things which are more important to you? That is, where does life come from, where does it go? What should you do this lifetime, why are we here? This is more important.

Now I have come to understand that all those psychic powers, all those spiritual powers, are only the by-products of meditation or *qi gong*. They appear because you have the potential. Everybody is a god, a part of God. Whatever power God has, you have. You are part of it. Your higher self is God, God is you. But now we don't realize that and separate ourselves from God. God, Buddha, the universe, Tao, to me it all means the same thing.

Now we have to work to pursue Tao, but Tao is not somewhere unreachable. It is right here under our feet. Everyday, whatever you do, whatever you think, whatever you say, it's right there. It is in daily life. Everything you are doing, twenty four hours a day, you are doing *qi gong*. Twenty four hours a day your are pursuing Tao. Tao is not outside there, so that I have to seek it outside my body. I don't have to go to the temple. Of course if you go to the temple perhaps you can be more quiet, you can be influenced by the discipline of that temple to help you in a way. But really, especially in the modern times, if everyone goes there who's going to feed your family? Who's going to take care of the society? So you should just stay where you are and pursue Tao every day.

Apart from that, you just do things to benefit other people. That is the essential thing for Buddhism and Taoism. You come here to help others and help yourself at the same time. This is the essential thing that we should do, become selfless. We have too much ego. Sometimes we are very selfish. If you can, get rid of the ego and purify yourself. Finally we say that we attain Tao. You have got nothing, except what you are. When you have reached that level you have really gained nothing! You have just gained your self. Now we are not what we used to be. We are so polluted. So it is a matter of getting rid of stuff like impurities, rather than getting something. Until finally you are so pure, like the original self, the higher self.

We come from nothing and we go back to nothing. It is really that we cannot see it that we call it nothing. It is everything. Like Tao. This is what we should work for. To me, the United States is so open, the people are much better prepared for the spiritual aspect. I see that many students are of very high consciousness and they have already done a lot of spiritual practice when they come to learn *qi gong*. I think that I can share some of my experiences but then when I talk with them I learn a lot. The American students have taught me more than I have taught them. It's a kind of exchange. It is true. The more I am with American students, the more I love them. At a certain level many students know much more than I do.

When I first came to the United States, the first two workshops that I did, in 1986, were in Arizona, then the third one was in New York. I talked about health the way I taught in China. Finally, a student asked me a question. "Professor Chen, you talked a lot about health. Do you want to leave our spirits alone?" I was really shocked. I realized I had made a mistake. I didn't dare to talk about spirituality. I did not know Americans very well. So she got me to thinking a lot. Ever since then, I have talked a lot about spiritual aspects. Now the first thing I talk about is the law of *qi gong*, about how we use the heart to contemplate the nothingness. This is *qi gong*. I think this is more important to tell people about in the very beginning.

Health is really connected to the body, which is a temporary temple. The soul lives in it, but who is feeling happy or unhappy? It is the spirit. Who is conducting your arms and legs? It is the spirit. This is the master, the one who is living in the house. It is not the house that is functioning, it is the master who is living there. That is eternal life. No matter how healthy you are, you are going to die. But if you are in poor health, the spirit is suffering. That is why it is very important to have good health. I used to be a very sick person and I want people to be healthy so they can contribute more, they can do more for others.

If you just sit there and talk about Buddhism and Taoism it doesn't mean anything. The most important thing you can do for people is to help them become aware of themselves, who they are, why they are here and what they should do. The major purpose of living this life is to learn how to go home, how to purify yourself and go home. This is our purpose of being thrown down here, or maybe we choose it.

Also, I think nowadays many people do not know what spiritual energy is but they care about their health. Sickness is a lesson. It's not a punishment, it's a lesson. You learn from the lesson and maybe this sickness will guide you onto the right path. I was guided onto this path by my cancer. If I had not had that then I would never have learned *qi gong*, I never had time, I was always busy, busy, busy.

I never thought I would be guided onto this path and become a teacher. When I was doing *qi gong* at the very beginning I had a very hard time. I was almost fifty years old at that time. Now I am sixty two and have such good energy. The *qi* itself really teaches you. When you are quiet the energy itself really comes. You can begin to understand many things. *Qi gong* itself teaches you because *qi* itself is the highest teacher. It is pure consciousness. It is the source of the universe. Of course it has wisdom. When you are quiet and on the same vibrational level with the *qi*, you get wisdom. You don't have to ask Professor this and Master that to teach you.

For me, I have not only learned from my masters but the most important way I have learned is from the people around me. The students, friends, children, even the trees and flowers. Sometimes I look at the flowers. They never charge me anything to look at them. They are so generous. The sun is so generous, passing its light to all people, poor or sick, rich, it does not matter who. If you are standing in the sun the sun is shining upon you, so generous. The wind, the rain, all of nature, so selfless. Can we be that selfless? We are not. If we can learn from the universe itself to become selfless, then we have attained Tao.

2

The Essence of Qi Gong

Yang Jwing-Ming

Dr. Yang Jwing Ming is well known in the world of *qi gong, tai ji,* and martial arts. He teaches and has developed centers all over the world. He lives, at least part of the year, in Boston, where he is president of Yang's Oriental Arts Association. Dr. Yang's words and teachings reflect a lifetime of serious practice (he has been involved with Chinese Wushu since 1961). At the same time, he is extremely humble and eager to impart what he has learned to serious students everywhere. He is the author of a number of books and videos on *tai ji, qi gong* and martial arts, published by Yang's Martial Arts Association (YMAA) in Jamaica Plain, Massachusetts.

You have classes here for people who do martial arts and also for people who just study qi gong and tai ji.

Yes.

Do you find that people are interested in learning one way instead of the other?

It depends. For instance, we have 10 schools in Poland. We have 700 students there. Before they were mainly interested in Shao Lin external style, but the last couple of years they have started getting into internal arts. We also have a school in Portugal and the main thing they are interested in there is external arts. In France they want half and half.

There is a problem in this country in that there are all kinds of people out there calling themselves qi gong masters, advertising themselves as such. And the public often has no way of knowing if they are bonafide or not.

People can say that they are a teacher of a certain style of *qi gong*, and that's really all that they can claim. I never want people to call me master, because in my definition of Master, that's almost like a Ph.D.. I still think of myself as being in high school. (laughter)

Well,the internal practices are something that do take a long time to develop.

Yes, they take a long time to understand and to comprehend, and to feel. Most of the people today may have knowledge from reading a book, but they are missing the comprehension and also the feeling. The feeling takes time to experience.

What do you mean by 'the feeling'?

The feeling you really have to go through like a meditation, such as the small circulation. You have to encounter all kinds of obstacles. Then you know how to solve a problem. My concern is that a good teacher has to comprehend the theory well enough that if he encounters some problem he can use his wisdom to analyze it and solve the problem.

People can learn a tai ji form in a matter of months. I mean, I've been doing the same tai ji form for four years now and I still feel like I'm a beginner. I feel I haven't yet reached that feeling that you were speaking of. In this country, it seems that people want to learn things really fast.

Yes, because they're modern people. This also includes becoming a master very fast. (laughter)

People want to learn a lot of different forms, so they can brag about how many forms they know.

Yes, but they never get deep. Now there's a big market. Some people only want to know enough of the form for their health. Unfortunately, there are not too many people who are really interested in getting to the essence of the art.

How would you describe this essence?

In order to know the essence you need to know about the deep theory, which usually takes about ten years minimum, to really comprehend and understand. Most people only want to study for two years then they say, 'OK, now I know it.' Then they think they can live forever! (laughter)
     The essence is actually the deep theory of the entire art. If people

don't know the theory then they can't develop. They have to be able to understand and analyze and then they can develop. That's why I say they have to be a Ph.D..

For example, you can sing the seven notes: do re me fa so la ti. The seven notes can become very classical, very deep and very touching emotionally. They can also be very shallow, like rock music and they can also make people excited. How many people today really appreciate classical music. Not too many, but when you go to a rock concert you can see thousands of people. It's the same with *tai ji*. With *tai ji* you have to think about how you play, if you want to play it like classical music you don't have a very big audience. If you play it like rock music, that's where the simplified forms come from, people can learn them easily.

These days I am more open minded. Now I see that in order to fit into today's society some people need the simplified forms. Among thirty or fifty people you may find one or two who are serious about the internal art.

The sad thing is, that in these modern days people are losing patience and they don't have such a strong will. I feel that it is important to preserve the art through writing and translating. It's like recording classical music, putting it on a tape and preserving it. *Yin* and *yang* have to change. When people get too much of the material side of life, sooner or later they will start to appreciate the yin side or the spiritual side. And when the time comes, at least they will have something in their hands they can read. That's why I appreciate the people who are qualified to write books or make something.

From what I understand, in Mainland China Taoism is not really known anymore. Young people have no idea who Lao Tzu or Chuang Tzu are.

Young people don't want to get involved in any kind of education or philosophy. They want everything to be modern. All those kinds of things that have taken thousands of years to develop they are not interested in, because they take time or you don't make money. But they'll come back, you'll see. In the last 10 years in American society there are more and more people already getting into the spiritual side of life over the material side.

Have you seen a difference since you've been here?

Oh yes. When I first came here in 1974 there was not much of a spiritual side. When you talked about *qi gong* or *qi*, people would look at you like you were a weirdo! (laughter) Now when you talk to people about *qi gong* they understand. People like meditation and *tai ji* has become more popular. Why, because of this baby boom generation. When these people start reaching forty they start getting back pain and start worrying about their health. When this generation gets to fifty and sixty, when they start getting older, if my prediction is right, the spiritual side will come out.

Do you think the same thing will happen in China?

Oh, I don't worry about China, because right now China follows America. When America gets into it then China will follow. Right now, the Chinese people, they don't even have their own dignity. They just put their own culture on the ground and step on it.

Actually, when I wrote the first few books I got a lot of phone calls and Chinese people wrote me letters and asked why was I sharing the secrets with Western people. I said to them, why not? They said that this was a Chinese treasure, we should not give it to outside people. I said well don't you understand, the Chinese, they put this treasure on the ground and stepped on it. So I just give it to people who will appreciate it.

Look at the Cultural Revolution in China. They destroyed all the culture. So if there is a foreign country who will appreciate this treasure and preserve it, I prefer to give it to them.

I feel that the education in this country needs to be reformed for the younger generation. For example, in my opinion, the younger generation needs to learn how to meditate. Their minds are outside of their bodies. We're talking about their material side, everything's material to them, like nintendo. The teachers now should be teaching the children right from the primary grades how to meditate, how to feel yourself, and how to feel nature.

Taoism, in China, is now a religion, with priests, and liturgy and ritual.

Yes, but the real Taoist philosophy and Taoist *qi gong* has been really abused by the Taoist monastery. It has become a superstition, like witchcraft. Now I see a lot of the *qi gong* masters in China who demonstrate some of the family *qi gong* style in a very low level.

I've been practicing your Eight Brocades practice. I find your books very clear and very easy to understand. The Eight Brocades is very simple, yet very nice.

It's good for beginners. It's very simple and straight forward. But for some people, it's too simple. They say to me that *qi gong* is supposed to be complicated. I say you're kidding. The highest *qi gong* is no movement. You just sit there! I think many people don't realize that *qi gong* can be simple and still be effective and helpful.

There are teachers out there now who are presenting these ancient Taoist practices in a very Western scientific way. Do you have any problem with that?

No, to me, if it's not scientific then it's no good.

You mean, if you don't present it in a way that Westerners can understand they won't respect it?

No, I mean that in order for people to respect it more you must tell them why they are doing it, instead of just giving them mysteries. Of course, a lot of things cannot be explained yet. Yet some can be. For example, how the *qi* circulates in the body in the channels, they can measure it now with equipment. They can measure the channel exactly, they can measure the current. Its just bio-electricity or electromagnetic waves. If you find an effective way to explain it then people will understand it.

So you don't try to present it just as something mystical.

No, if you present it as something mystical you will get some people interested but that way you aren't building the foundation for the practical research. What I try to do is build the scientific foundations and try to relate it to the medical science. In the last fifteen years, we have moved from medical science to energy science. Before it was all based only what you could see but now they believe in what you feel.

Do you feel you have a certain role here in the Western culture? Do you feel you have something that you're bringing here?

Yes, I believe that I was put here to build a bridge. This bridge is to try and transfer Chinese culture into Western Culture. The second thing is that he wants me to preserve the arts in the Western society.

The thing I like about your style is that you are not interested in just teaching people the outer forms. It seems very important to you that they do get the essence.

You see, with every five hundred people you may find three or four. But that's okay. You don't want a hundred masters. (laughter) Any student that comes must conquer themselves first, before they can get deeper.

What do you feel Taoist philosophies and practices have for the West?

Taoist practices are different from Buddhist ones. The Buddhist really tries to escape from the layman society completely. They would go high in the mountains for their cultivation to become a Buddha. Modern Taoism has been heavily influenced by Buddhism. Before Buddhism came to China, Taoism was what is called scholarly Taoism, in which people were looking for a peaceful life. That is what Lao Tzu's *Tao Te Ching* is about. Then, after 50 AD, when Buddhism entered China, Zhang Dao Ling combined the Buddhist theory and the traditional Taoist theory and created what we now think of as religious Taoism.

Religious Taoism is a combination of the tradition of hiding in the mountains and at the same time trying to stay in the world or the layman's society. That way it is easier for people to accept Taoism than Buddhism. After two thousand years of development, Taoism has been more accepted by the lay person's society than Buddhism because in Buddhism you really have to enter the mountains. As a Taoist you can get married, you can have sex, you can eat meat, and at the same time you can cultivate. This means that is that it is much easier for Taoism to be adapted into Western society.

Now a lot of Buddhism has entered Western society and people are concentrating on the philosophy instead of the practice. Understanding the philosophy is one thing, how much you really practice is another. In Taoism, you can practice at the same time as studying the philosophy, because Taoism doesn't separate them.

For example, when you train in *qi gong,* you have to emphasize both the physical body and the *qi* body. In Buddhism, they don't care about the physical body. They only want to use the *qi* body to nourish the brain for enlightenment. That's the only thing they're looking for. That's why Buddhism is not practical.

Taoist theory is different from Buddhism. Taoist theory says that in order to become the Buddha, or to reach enlightenment, you need to have a long life. Taoists try to achieve longevity by maintaining a good healthy body. This has become a very important part of the difference between Buddhism and Taoism. In Taoism we emphasize health and longevity *qi gong* practice. Actually, you can see today in most of the *qi gong* documents they are really not talking about enlightenment. The emphasis is more on longevity and health, which is why Taoism is much easier for the average person to relate to.

There was a tradition in Taoism of people going into the mountains to cultivate.

Yes, they do go to the mountains. Yet at the same time, they can get married and have children.

Some of the other teachers I've been speaking with emphasize that today's Taoism needs to have more people practicing in society and fewer people going to the mountains to become hermits.

Yes, the reason for that is very simple. It is that, traditionally, Taoists tried to separate from society so that they would not have any emotional bondage. One way to find a peaceful life is to not have any emotional disturbance. That way you can reach a high level of cultivation. But today, there is no difference, the mountain and the society are the same. You cannot hide. Even in the mountains, there is no place for you to hide.

The second thing is that if I go to the mountains to cultivate, how much achievement can I get? The amount would be very low because I don't have access to the documents and the knowledge that has already been revealed to the public. Here, in my hand, I have so much material that has been revealed from the past, that it will direct me to the direct path and shorten my training time.

Remember that Tao is the natural way. The natural way of human life is not hiding in the mountains. You need to marry, have children and then from there you find the way of life.

The challenges are very different when you live in the world than when you're away from society.

Right.

Do you feel that Taoist practices work differently in the West than in China?

Somewhat, because it is a different culture. The first thing is that in China, students will follow the practices without any questions. In Western society they have lots of questions. Remember that in China, for every twenty people who join the monastery for training, at least ten or fifteen will finish. In Western society, if you get one you'll be lucky.

Another big difference is that Western society is looking for a logical or scientific explanation. In China they are following the tradition and whatever the master says they will obey exactly. Western society will put a question mark there until they can get a logical explanation.

Do you think that's a good or bad thing?

The best way is for a student to be loyal to the teacher. That is what's missing in Western society.

The problem that we have found in the West is that sometimes teachers have abused their power. Students who just blindly follow the teacher can be mislead.

In China, also a lot of teachers abuse their power. That's why today in Western society, students have the opportunity to see which teacher is good, and which teacher is not good. Now, each teacher has to reveal their knowledge. Once they find a good teacher then they study with them. At the same time, the Chinese master does not usually have an easy time teaching in this society because they are scared that the students will betray them. So many students in America are going around calling themselves Master. Many of them don't even practice themselves, how can they call themselves Master? This kind of thing discourages traditional Chinese Masters to teach American students.

In China, the student's loyalty is always the first thing emphasized. However, at the same time, the Chinese students don't develop, they don't think for themselves out of loyalty to the teacher. They also don't find other sources. For example, *qi gong*, as an art, should be absorbed from many sources.

The good thing about the typical American way is that people need to keep an open mind and keep learning from everywhere. Unfortunately, some people learn for a short time and they claim to be a Master. That's why I say that there are pros and cons to each approach.

How can Westerners know when a teacher is bona fide or not? We don't have a tradition here to refer to.

That's exactly why it's so hard. There is that cultural difference. At the same time, I am so curious. When I look at Japanese people who come to this county to teach karate and so on, they are very traditional. I see Americans bowing to the Master and between the Master and student they keep a good distance. In their tradition, the teacher gets so much respect. Yet when the teacher gets too close to the students they start betraying them. The human mind is very funny. The more easy-going you become the easier it is to be betrayed.

I don't say that I am a Master, because I feel that I am just starting to understand. When the students are looking for a teacher, there are a few guidelines that they can follow. The first is if the teacher practices himself or is he just talking. I have seen many teachers who talk more than they practice. How can they tell the students to practice hard?

The second thing is if the teacher continues searching and studying. The Tao is so great. You can spend ten lifetimes studying it without learning it all. How can you say you're satisfied with your knowledge? It's impossible.

The third thing is how much does the teacher know scientifically? Is his mind very stubborn in a traditional way or is his mind open, so that he can really listen to other people? Does he try to talk with other people and learn a modern explanation for the teachings? Or does he just say that modern science cannot explain it?

Number four is how much does the teacher want to share with you? Is he sharing from the heart? Is he willing to share his knowledge with you or is he holding back? The teacher who says, "Give me two thousand dollars and I will give you a little secret." It's not worth it!

The best way to find a teacher is one who has published books. I don't say that just because I have published books. But if he can publish books then usually that means that his understanding is pretty profound. Read his book and see how much he really understands.

It's not the same as ancient times. In ancient times, teachers taught by word of mouth and it could take three years to find out that the teacher is no good and abusive. You've wasted years. Today's communication is so good. You can use it.

What is the best way for Westerners to approach these practices?

The best way to do it is to search out the good books and read them and get a basic understanding. There are so many ways that a Taoist can train, right? This way you can set up the course in whatever direction you want to go. Too many people just blindly jump in and then every six months they change, here and there and get nowhere. It's not really their fault, but they do not know how to begin.

As you mentioned before, there are people who just study Lao Tzu, Chuang Tzu, and the philosophy. But what's so important about Taoism is that the practice is such an integral part. You can't just read books and know the philosophy, you must have a practice and make it part of your life.

You have to combine the philosophy and the practice. One is reality and one is only dreaming. When you put them together then your life has meaning.

How has being in the West affected your practice and your approach to teaching?

When I first came to this country, in 1974, on my face I had a big, heavy, thick mask. That mask was created by Chinese tradition. Everything I did, I did the Chinese way. For example, if the students were late I wouldn't even talk to them. Then later, I realized that this is a different society, a different culture. I had to force myself slowly to accept this culture. It was very difficult. I was trained in the traditional way, so it was difficult for me to open my mind and say that I would share my knowledge with the American students, because I didn't trust them.

The good side though, of the Western culture, is that people have an open mind and they can discuss things. Knowledge should be shared instead of held inside. From them, I learned that I had to open my mind if I wanted to live in this society. I learned to take my mask off, layer by layer. The more I adjusted myself, the more I began to fit into this society.

At one time, I adjusted too much and I got so close to the students that I didn't get any respect from them. They treated me like shit! Then I had to adjust and find a middle way, half Chinese, half American.

Do you feel you have a role or mission to bring these practices to the West?

About twenty years ago, when I first came to this country, I realized that about ninety five per cent of Chinese martial arts were really American style Chinese martial arts. Most of them seemed based on the Bruce Lee motion pictures. Very few of the movements were practical. It's almost like American style Chinese food. It doesn't taste right.

My first mission then was to direct the American people, because so many of them had been mislead. It was not their fault. There were no guidelines, or good books, and few good teachers. That's why I started writing books in 1979, because hopefully, through the books I can direct people onto the right path.

Then I realized that people were interested in *qi gong* but they treated it like so much of a mystery or a mystical thing. Chinese *qi gong* has existed for over four thousand years. It's a higly devloped human spiritual science. My mission is to help society by teaching *qi gong.*

I think a lot of Westerners romanticize China, like in the old Kung Fu television series, but what the people in China want is the material side. They may practice qi gong for health but they don't study Lao Tzu anymore.

In China, you see, they have always had the spiritual side. They are so poor and to them Americans are all so rich. Now they have the opportunity to become rich and all that's on their mind is money. Nobody wants to train *kung fu* any more or cultivate themselves. The only reason they try to become a Taoist or to learn *qi gong* is to earn money. They can come to the United States and become famous!

Americans, on the other hand, are turning from the material side to the spiritual side, while at the same time China is turning from the spiritual side to the material side. This world has to flip around.

Yin yang.

Yes, *yin yang.* That's why Chinese people have put Chinese culture on the ground.

It seems as though it's starting to come back a little though. Qi gong is very popular now in China. When I was there last year, the teachers that I met talked a lot about spiritual cultivation.

There are many good *qi gong* books published in mainland China now. I have some published by the Chinese government that are very good. But I'm talking about the majority of the layman-type people.

Too often people try to treat *qi gong* like some strange mystical thing. In my opinion, in order to really promote human life into higher levels of understanding, we really have to raise up the spiritual side. The spiritual side of cultivation has been studied in China for four thousand years.

I wonder if at some point the tradition will become so strong in the West that people from here will have to go back and teach people in China.

Now the Chinese people are learning the material side, and the Americans are learning the wisdom from China. My prediction is that fifty years from now China will come to America to learn the spiritual side.

3
Cultivating the Garden

Maoshing Ni

Author, lecturer, and licensed practitioner of Traditional Chinese Medicine, Dr. Maoshing Ni, Ph.D., D.O.M., is the co-founder and Vice President of Yo San University of Traditional Chinese Medicine in Santa Monica, California. Born and raised in a family medical tradition that spans many generations, Maoshing Ni studied Chinese Medicine and Taoist arts with his father, Hua Ching Ni. Dr. Ni has lectured and taught workshops throughout the country on such diverse subjects as longevity, preventative medicine, Chinese therapeutic nutrition, Chinese herbal medicine, physiognomy/facial readings, *Feng Shui/* geomancy, acupuncture, *tai ji, qi gong,* stress management and the history of medicine. His latest book, a translation of the *Yellow Emperor's Classic on Medicine,* has been published by Shambhala Publications. Both his depth of knowledge and his easy-going manner illustrate his long-term study and personal involvement in the Taoist arts.

One of the reasons I was interested in speaking with you is because you are someone who is bridging civilizations here, coming from a long line of very traditional teachers and healers, and here you are working and teaching in the West. Do you feel that your role is to bring the ancient traditional teachings into a modern Western perspective so that people here can use them?

Yes, very much so. As a matter of fact, I regard my life's mission as precisely that. First to able to take this really wonderful, useful knowledge that will be lost if we don't preserve it. Number two, even if we preserve it, if we don't present it and communicate it in a way that modern societies can utilize, we also lose it. That's very much how I view my mission in life, to be able to bridge this gap and to bring about an exchange in both directions. We must look at how, in every civilization there is useful wisdom. Despite the grossly materialistic trend that Western society has moved towards, there are areas that have been of benefit for humankind. So we must look at both ways. We must look at an exchange between the East and the West. The goal here is to form a global harmony.

From what I understand, the spiritual aspects of Taoism have all but died out in China. So, that's a whole other area that will need to be reawakened in some way.

Yes, but what's interesting is this, though, if you recall that *qi gong* as a phenomenon really started in China in the early 1970's. It swept through China very quickly and became a very popular practice.

Primarily for health.

Yes, primarily for health. But in some ways, it's really a disguised form of spiritual yearning. Instead of talking about a religion or a tradition, they talk about the health benefits of the practice. So, in some ways, China has naturally attempted to keep part of the tradition. What you are seeing now is the society opening up and people are now actually turning to religion. Catholicism, Buddhism, Taoism, folk Taoism that is, have begun to slowly take root. As communism falls to the wayside, people are looking for another system, like religion. Unfortunately, I think that the esoteric traditions like ours will always remain with only a small handful of people.

I have this feeling that historically the pure Taoism of Lao Tzu and Chuang Tzu, the true independent spiritual Taoists, have always been in the minority. At least for the last few centuries, many more people have been drawn to folk Taoism. For many people, true spiritual freedom is just too heavy a responsibility. So they look towards something that can give them a belief system. Do you find that true in this country?

I find it refreshing that in this country there are actually more people who are interested in spiritual independence. Therefore, they are becoming very open to these new ideas. We saw a wave in the sixties and seventies in the hippie era where people weren't so independent. They were looking for gurus. In recent times, the last decade or so, I have encountered more and more people who are interested in taking responsibility for their lives and helping others.

An example would be the environmental movement. The environmental activists, and this is my perception of it, are very concerned about this global destruction that civilization has brought about. So their interest is to try to help restore human's existence with his or her environment. In a very gross way, that is very much a Taoist principle. While I don't approve of some of the tactics that are being used, nevertheless, the concept and theories are very much in concert with Taoism.

So we have the first wave of people who have come out and spoken out about the need for harmonization. I think that as this trend continues more and more people will begin to turn their attention towards their own lives. It's much easier to look outside and try to fix something outside of yourself, such as the environment. It's much harder to turn inward and try to fix what's inside of you.

Taoism seems to usually have been about a good balance of both.

Yes, indeed.

One of the things that I noticed in the 60's and 70's was that lots of us went to the other extreme. So many people were going inward and just forgetting about the outward.

Giving up a practical life.

Yes, with some misconceptions about Eastern mysticism also. People thinking that we needed to be ascetics and suffer or it was better to be poor, and it's holier to be thin and half-starved, all that sort of thing. Also with the gurus, there were abusive situations that happened. I think that people are a little more ready to take responsibility for themselves. One of the terms I like the most is self-cultivation.

The image is so much like a garden, where, unless you tend to it and nourish it and continually till the soil, you will only get what you put into it.

So you must be pretty busy; maintaining a private practice, running the school and an herb company.

I have lots of help. I couldn't to do it by myself. We have wonderful people that work with us. I think the most important thing is that because we have a mission, and we operate by very special principles that others also identify and believe in, that's what makes it all happen. The power of the individual is limited. Looking back, I think that what my father has been trying to do is to first, help people awaken themselves to their potentials and to begin to cultivate people's potentials individually. Now he sees that the next phase is to be able to go out and help others in order to make our society or make our world a little better place. You can sit on the mountain top and become a *hsein* or immortal from years of practice, but if you leave the world in a worse place than you came to it then in some way you have not fulfilled your service. There are two parts. One is self cultivation, the other is service. Service to the world.

Now how does one get involved in working in service to the world without becoming caught up in the anger and the frustration in dealing with world conditions?

I think that you cannot come from a place of anger. If you come from a place of anger it will kill you instantly. There are many things to be angry about, but it's not about that. It's about first balancing your life and doing a little bit more each time in whatever capacity in your immediate world that you can do, short of going on a starvation fast until someone changes the policy. That's extreme. Taoism doesn't promote extreme behavior.

Rather, on a daily basis, do a little bit more. It could be as simple as helping a friend out. It could be sending a book to a prisoner. It could be participation in local community activities where it can bring some benefits. It could be going to an elementary school or a junior high school to give a speech to young eager minds who are open and want to learn more about alternatives and options, compared to what is traditional here in America.

There are many things that one can do according to one's own capacity, on a daily basis. One doesn't need to give up one's life to go into service. Rather, service occurs every moment, in every day.

Do you feel that there's an attitude adjustment that one can use to go into the world to be of service without being caught up in it, to be "in the world but not of it"?

I think that taking the guidance of the *Tao Te Ching* which advises you to be like water, always nurturing, but in the lowest position. In whatever way that you see that you are capable of doing, you contribute, keeping a balance. You can take service to the extreme. I know of a person who is very religious and who has basically renounced family obligations and so forth to go into service for a religious organization and become a full-time volunteer and recruiter. This is extreme behavior. Even though the service is something that he or she may believe in very much, by not fulfilling their basic responsibility to their family, children, spouse and so forth it's too extreme. There needs to be balance.

That's one of the things that drew me to Taoism in the beginning. That feeling of groundedness and balance, that it's not an extreme position. There isn't one diet for everyone, one particular practice for everyone, one attitude for everyone. Rather, we take into consideration the various types of individuals and stages in life and times in life.

Yes, because we're all very uniquely different individuals. Our basic natures are the same. So we can say there's a universal truth or law that governs all, but at the same time within this truth it takes on a very individual expression. So, as you say, diets are different. If you take two people, who live in two different climates, who do two different kinds of work, even though they're the same age, the same build, the same genetic background and so forth—the requirements are a little different. So you have to make that variation accordingly.

The important thing for people is to develop themselves so that they have this awareness and become in tune to what they need. Initially, they can be guided by someone knowledgeable, like a doctor of Chinese medicine, but beyond a certain point, you try to become self sufficient. Again, that is not to reject any help that one should seek when it is necessary, for it is very important as part of one's development and one's learning.

In what other ways would you recommend that people work on their development?

I think that one of the most important things is to not lose sight of certain principles. I think these principles need to be practiced on a daily basis and these are the principles of the *Tao Te Ching* and the *I Ching*. By practicing these principles one can have a very clear vision and understanding of what one's life is about. In our tradition we offer the various spiritual practices—invocations, meditation, *qi gong,* *tai ji chuan,* eight treasures, *dao in*—these are just samples of some of the practices that are available.

Then, to continually learn about the practical knowledge of life; by that I mean health, longevity, diet and mental attitude. Finally, to become of service, that part of it also becomes a very important tool to help one's cultivation.

You come from a tradition of people who worked as doctors and also taught as spiritual teachers. Do you see yourself in that role?

I see myself as a healer. I think healer is a very broad term, because a healer encompasses a teacher—on a physical, emotional and spiritual plane. The way I look at my healing work, and the way that we teach our students at Yo San University, is that we teach them to become true healers. What that means is that when a patient comes in and they have obvious physical sufferings we relieve them of the physical sufferings. However, they also have emotional sufferings as well. We help them by giving them proper counsel. Therefore, I think that the most important part of a healer's job is not merely to relieve physical suffering, but to help teach the patient, the individual, so that they can begin to heal their own lives. So that when they go home they can think about and experience some of the changes that are happening and then they can begin to see their lives more clearly and get a better sense of what they should do. Then they go about making those changes in their lives and bring about more peace and tranquillity and happiness. So what we're doing here is we're healing people's lives and not simply healing their aches and pains.

It's very different than just going in and taking care of their low kidney energy or their damp spleen or their aches and pains.

Why do they have the low kidney energy? Perhaps they're working fourteen hours a day and driving four hours a day. In other words, we need to help them change their lives, help them transform, be a positive instrument to help them become creative and make changes that can be beneficial. Then, when we heal these individuals, they go on to heal themselves further. They effect their friends, their family members and so forth, and you see the rippling effect moving outwards. Down the road we can have a major impact.

So a healer takes the role of a teacher, a friend, an advisor, a doctor, and also a student. Every day I learn something from my patients. They equally give me back what I give them, and it enriches my life in so many ways. The type of work that I'm doing is very satisfying and at the same time I teach my students not to lose sight of the ultimate impact that they can have on the world at large.

I like that idea of the rippling effect. You're not just treating a patient, you're treating their whole family in that way.

That's right.

I was thinking about the work that all you folks are doing down there—I mean how do you feel about being in L.A.? Talk about being in the middle of the hardest-core American materialistic culture, home of the earthquakes, and all that. Do you think that has any effect on your work?

I think it's a perfect opportunity to practice the Taoist principles of being unshakable, right? (laughter) When the world shakes around you and it's hard, when its rough out there, you try to remain still and calm and clear in your vision and your mission. We find that Los Angles is a good place because people are open. In general, its a good community that is very open to changes.

In the midst of all the craziness and the wonderfulness of Western civilization, where do you see Taoism as having its place? Where do these traditions and practices fit in this culture?

I believe that it will become widely available. If you examine what is available in today's bookstores, you have the Tao of everything now.

It's obvious to me that if these books are finding their way into bookstores then people are buying them, they're instructed, they're intrigued by this whole new philosophy, whole new paradigm of the Tao. The Tao is also very flexible, very adaptive. So it doesn't matter if it's even called the Tao ultimately. The most important thing is that people begin to see, understand and practice its principles so that their lives can become much more positive, much more creative, and much more gratifying.

In some ways I feel that right now Taoism is sort of like Buddhism was in the 70's in this county it was really starting to take hold. Now we see a very wide-spread Buddhist community in this country that's doing all sorts of wonderful work in prisons and hospitals. It's not just people going on meditation retreats. It's really entered into a lot of people's lives.

When you're beginning to have an impact on actual community then you're basically distilling the essence of these philosophies and bringing them into people's daily lives. That's where it really counts. These meditation retreats are wonderful, but as soon as you leave the meditation retreat, you're liable to forget it all.

Right now in this country, like in China, we're seeing a growing interest in qi gong. And, like in China, a lot of people are approaching it from the standpoint of health, which is fine. But like you were saying, I don't think it's possible to seriously practice qi gong without it starting to have spiritual benefits, whether or not that's what you're looking for or even understand. Things are going to start happening. Then, that's a whole other level that people have to learn to start working with. I think the beauty of the Taoist teachings, as a whole, is that some of the most powerful practices are the simplest.

Precisely.

That's another thing that we can offer people. We're not in-

volving them in a lot of long, complicated rituals. You don't have to renounce your family or even your religion. You can be a practicing Catholic or Buddhist or Jew or whatever and do qi gong or work with Chinese herbs or even meditation.

I have seen how this can all fit together. We've talked about the different components. The way that we can offer service—I offer my personal medical service to patients and when patients become healthy and I send them on their way they must find a way to keep themselves in balance. I teach them. We have classes and so forth to teach them about *qi gong*, nutrition, self care, and give them books to read from which they can heal themselves and at the same time offer them another option, which is the food herbs. The food herbs become very important in this regard, because they can use the food herbs to maintain their balance and help themselves. It becomes a tool for those interested in spiritual cultivation, and they can use the herbs to support their *jing*, support their *qi* and to support their *shen*. It can act as an additional support and fuel for the cultivation that they do.

In many Taoist stories and legends the teacher finds the student. They will often test the student by asking them to swallow some kind of repulsive, poisonous substances, which are really disguised food herb formulations. Once they've passed the test and proven their sincerity, then the teacher becomes willing to teach them. At the same time, because of the herbs they've taken, they have already been prepped, so to speak. In other words, it has already built their foundation. They can already learn advanced practices. This has been an esoteric tradition.

That brings to mind this idea that Taoist self cultivation includes qi practices, herbs, and medical knowledge as well as self cultivation. In this country most people only study tai ji or only TCM. It's all been broken up. Some people study only Tao Te Ching or scholarly applications of Chuang Tzu or something. I think it's really important to start putting all these things back together again so that people can understand that it can effect their lives in so many different ways.

Specialization is very much a Western approach. The Eastern paradigm is beginning to have a positive influence in America. So, too, Americans are beginning to see the benefits of holism, to be able to put the whole picture together. Looking at the planet at large, people are starting to say 'hey, if we dump this chemical into this river it flows down and destroys trees and we have less oxygen and it goes on and on.' It's the ripple effect, a chain reaction that occurs at every level. So look at the whole picture. Then you can begin to see very clearly what you need to do to help restore the balance. As a classical healer you must have the whole picture. If you have just one or two then you're incomplete.

You are a practitioner of Traditional Chinese Medicine. It seems to me that that is one of the first places that a lot of people come to the teachings of Tao, as patients.

Certainly, many of the students of Tao have begun as patients. They are first exposed to Chinese thought through Chinese Medicine. It's a whole new way of looking at health. Then, after experiencing positive results in their health, they begin to look at how this philosophy can benefit their lives. From there, they begin to take classes in *tai ji, qi gong, dao in,* and so on. They become intrigued because of the effects of *qi.* Then they can begin to take classes in the *I Ching,* the classic *Book of Changes,* and how they can use that to help themselves spiritually and emotionally, as well as learning about environmental influences through *feng shui.*

What do you think are the strengths of Chinese medicine as opposed to what we think of as Western medicine?

Western medicine is very reductionist and very fragmented and only looks at a small part of the body at the expense of the rest. Whereas Chinese medicine is a holistic medicine, encompassing the entire body. Each cell relates with another cell, with another organ, with another system. So everything is interlinked. Beyond that, the person's relationship with his or her family, social environment, living environment, their job, their mind and emotional states are all connected. I'm tempted to use the term ecological medicine to describe Chinese medicine. It is very much the ecology of the human body with his or her environment.

Do you feel that Chinese medicine has certain strengths and even weaknesses?

I believe that its strength lies in its ability to view the whole picture, and therefore advising people to make changes that will benefit them, not just currently, but also years down the road. So, when they make that shift, then everything falls into place. That's the strength of Chinese medicine. It's a long range plan.

In terms of shortcomings, I think that the shortcoming that is inherent within Chinese medicine in that it is a difficult medicine to master. The cure that you render varies from practitioner to practitioner, depending on your understanding and grasp of the medicine. Unlike Western medicine, which is very systematic, where there are specific procedures to follow and such, Chinese medicine's weakness lies in the unevenness in the kind of care that is given.

That's interesting, because my next thought was about how there's a way to practice Chinese medicine that's a very straightforward TCM which can be very mechanical. Or you can bring in a whole other element, with the Taoist practices and philosophy.

Yes, if they're trained that way, if they're exposed to the entire school of thought, instead of just a partial and narrow path. If you follow a narrow path you will tend to miss something.

When I was in China last summer, we had some qi gong practitioners come to do some demonstrations for us. One doctor had a patient come by who had a heart condition. He applied both needling and just "shooting" qi into the patient in his treatment. What I thought was an interesting component of the treatment plan was that the doctor taught the patient a

simple qi gong practice that he could do for himself. Here in the West, even with Chinese medicine, people still have the idea that they are going to a practitioner so that they can be cured.

That's where Chinese medicine differs from the Western approach in that we engage the patients as partners. We act very much as healers and educators. We are teachers, so we teach the patient about the principles, about things that they can do, about practices that they can do to help themselves. We engage their partnership in this healing process as opposed to a one-way street, "Pop this pill and call me in the morning" type of thing. There's no responsibility there.

So you think that that's important, then, to bring in these other elements of healing besides just the acupuncture and herbs?

Absolutely. Otherwise you will have missed a great gift. If you practice Chinese medicine as it's practiced now in China, it's a very mechanical approach, not that dissimilar to Western medicine. You just dispense herbs and put needles in people and that's it. You need to become their confidante, their teacher, their advisor, their friend, as well as their doctor.

Some practitioners may feel that's too much to take on.

That's a big responsibility. We certainly let people choose how they want to practice. That's why there's inconsistancies within the profession of Chinese medicine. I think that it can be a weakness, but it can also be a strength The strength is that there are people who choose to go beyond the mechanical practice of TCM and really bring the whole ecology of medicine into play.

Didn't what was originally called Classical Chinese Medicine involve eight or nine branches, including qi gong, meditation, diet, feng shui, astrology, and things like that?

Very much so. In today's time these things have become fragmented. In China, acupuncturists are specialists, they don't dispense herbs. *Tui na* doctors do *tui na*. It's very fragmented now, which is unfortunate, because all the tools can be gathered under one person to be utilized for the benefit of the patient. This is why Chinese medicine can treat a wider variety of conditions than Western medicine. Today, if you have five conditions you have to see five specialists and they don't even communicate with each other.

Under Chinese medicine, however, you can integrate it all under one roof. You can work with the big picture and the primary cause, which began the domino effect. You then seek to restore the balance.

You need to become balanced and well rounded. Certainly you can become an expert in a certain field. That is a nice gift. I think that's a personal accomplishment and achievement. However, sometimes by becoming an expert in one thing, you forsake the opportunity to help balance your knowledge. For instance, in the scholarly tradition, someone who fully focuses on a very narrow specialty, their mind becomes narrow as well. Then they lose the capacity to be open and encompassing.

What would be your definition of true health? In the West we think of true health as the absence of symptoms.

I don't think there is a limit to how well you can feel. In the definition of Chinese medicine it is an abundance of *jing* and *qi* and the ability to feel inner peace and serenity of *shen*. How that would manifest is not only a sense of well being but having great energy, not hyper energy, but a calm sort of serene energy, and having stamina that can be called upon when necessary.

I think true health is reflected in how well one integrates one's mind and body and spirit. If that is all in concert then you have true health. If any one part is out of synch, your mind will be racing ahead and your body will be falling behind, which happens a lot in our modern society. It happens with people who work in offices or people who over-exert their physical body and don't develop their mind as well at that same time. Again, when you're integrated and in harmony and in concert then you can experience not only an absence of symptoms but a true sense of wellness.

Another subject that I'd like to bring up is that of death and dying. There's been a lot of information coming out from Buddhist traditions lately, but I haven't seen too much on that subject in Taoist books. What is the death experience and how can we help people who are going through that?

In the Taoist tradition, the emphasis of course, has always been focused on being alive every moment. That's why we have not put so much emphasis and focus on death. Though certainly, death has been discussed and explored for centuries in the Taoist tradition.

However, death is such an insignificant event to a Taoist. It is simply a transformation of one energy to another, which one does one's whole life anyway, constantly transforming. So the understanding of the natural law of transformation makes death a very natural process and therefore not a big deal.

To a Taoist, death needs to be a natural process and a dignified one, and not what we have in the Judeo-Christian traditions of death. Oftentimes we find the brutality of Western medicine really causing a very degrading death. They may consider it a heroic measure to put people on life support for a month, two months, a year or even two years. What does that serve? Does it serve their family? Does it serve the individual spirit? It can cause more suffering on both ends. In the Taoist tradition we try not to interfere with nature. What that means is that naturally death will come knocking at your door, when the qi is exhausted and the *shen* is ready to depart and *jing* is no longer present. A TCM doctor will be able to recognize when this is happening and not interfere and prolong unnecessary suffering in the last moments of one's life.

What about the view of reincarnation, which a lot of people understand as a personality that goes from one lifetime to another, learning lessons until they reach a divine state. The Taoists look at reincarnation a little differently, don't they?

We still recognize the recycling of the *qi*.

So we're not talking about a personality then?

We're not talking about a personality. We're talking about the *qi* that is simply transformed. I think the most basic physical law is that energy cannot be destroyed, but can only be transferred or transformed. It is transformed into different manifestations. So we have this qi that scatters and is transformed into the next reincarnation.

Reincarnation, in Taoist tradition is a natural concept as well. The *shen*, or the consciousness, leaves at the time of the death of the body. If the *shen* is not cultivated, then that *shen* will basically be drawn back into the big melting pot and then will become attracted to the next manifestation, whatever that may be.

Which may or not be a human?

Which may not. Nevertheless, I think that the whole idea of cultivation is to be able to learn to gather your *qi* and solidify your *qi* and your *shen* to such a degree that you gain control and mastery over it, so that you can achieve this spiritual immortality that we talk about.

So that a bigger package is then passed on?

There's a wholeness. That is why achieved people can have a knowledge of their own past. Their spirit never scatters and their qi never goes back into the universal energy pot. They carry on and continue and so there is an idea or concept that in each generation or manifestation they continue their work. The ultimate idea here is to achieve liberation and independence, so that you can become a *hsein*, an immortal or realized being.

Would one be in a body or not in a body at that point?

You wouldn't need a human body at that point because the spirit has solidified to such a degree that it's an independent, intelligent and conscious being.

Then are they able to help seekers or students who are working on their own cultivation?

They can be of service or they can simply move to a whole new dimension of existence. We only know of the physical dimension, because of our senses. We are limited by these senses. There are other dimensions of existence that we're completely unaware of.

So what can we do for people who are facing death, to perhaps help them with their struggle?

The person who is dying, at this point in life, struggles in a futile attempt to live. We must at first help them to become peaceful, to help them regain that inner peace before they die.

To some people, it may not be a peaceful feeling to think that perhaps they have not done enough cultivation and they're just going off into the melting pot. For some people, reincarnation almost seems like another chance.

I think that no matter what you've done with your life, at the end you just need to let it go, and be peaceful and okay about it. It's important to help people to learn to forgive, forgive themselves and other people. That's very important. And to help them plant the seed so that when they do reincarnate into another generation or another being they can have that seed that grows within them to refine themselves and cultivate themselves.

So you're saying it's never too late.

Yes. You can start cultivating at any point. Your life is like the seasons; when spring passes then we have summer, fall, and finally winter arrives. That's the dying. Then there's a period of dormant stillness. But there always will be another spring. Spring will come again and there's a rebirth, so that seed which lies dormant in the winter time under snow, will germinate and blossom again and begin the whole process anew.

That is why, I guess, that Taoists identify so much with nature. They say that you can't go wrong with nature.

Nature is a mirror. It's the mirror of the natural law. We observe nature in order to see.

From your viewpoint as a practitioner, as an instructor of qi gong, and as a lifelong cultivator, do you see a unique or perhaps different form of what we might call American Taoism emerging, or is it too soon to tell yet?

The Tao has always worn many coats throughout history, sometimes to conceal itself or its essence, such as in the secret traditions. At other times it has been promoted in a very commercialized way. I don't think that in the West it's going to be any different. Our hope is that we will be able to preserve the essence of Tao, no matter what clothes it wears. We will preserve the essence so that people can utilize the knowledge and apply it.

Again, the wisdom of the Tao is such that the term Tao doesn't really describe any of it. As Lao Tzu pointed out, it's very difficult to describe this thing called Tao. As soon as you talk about the Tao you conceptualize it and then it has lost its true experience and meaning. It becomes an intellectual process. Our hope is to be able to distill at least some of its essential parts that can be applied, using the Western delivery system, which is communication, so that we can do a better job to convey this to the public. Under the Chinese historical system, it has been clouded in metaphors and has not been a direct teaching. It has been a teaching that you have had to really search for, that you had to really spend years of your life studying.

I think students today are much more privileged, in that the information is so much more readily available to them. They don't realize how difficult it was to gather and preserve this knowledge over the years. Now, we suddenly have the availability of it all at our fingertips, this time-tested wisdom of a thousand years. This is an exciting era when we can indeed make this available because people are open and they are ready to make a commitment to change their lives for the better, and help us make a better world.

4
The Perfect Square Has No Corners
Lily Siou

Lily Siou began studying at the age of six at the Tai Hsuan Monastery in Kiangsi Province which was established in 210 B.C.E. on Lung Hu Shan, the mountain of the dragon and the tiger. There, she was trained in *qi gong*, ritual observances, music, calligraphy and Chinese medicine. She now lives in Hawaii where she has founded the Tai Hsuan Foundation College of Acupuncture and Herbal Medicine. In addition to her practice as a doctor of Chinese medicine, she teaches *qi gong* and is the 64th generation Master of the Cheng I Taoist School in China. Small, yet extremely energetic and strong, Dr. Siou radiates both calmness and a controlled power accumulated from long years of practice.

How long have you been teaching in the West now?

Twenty five years.

So you've really seen the Western students' progress?

They are very sincere. Some of them extend themselves even more than the Chinese, but they don't have enough background to be able to understand the foundation. It is a little bit harder for them to understand how the perfect square has no corners.

I don't know that one either!

It means everything can be in perfect order, but you have to be more round about things. You must be quite adaptable without going all over the place. You must be very creative and very scientific but be able to understand that the corner has no angle.

A sort of focused flexibility?

Tao is the main focus, the center itself of the universe, which produces all life or forms.

So the idea behind these practices is that people want to be able to identify and work with the original source of all qi or life — Tao, correct?

If a person can connect their internal self to the root of Tao, then they can gain immortality, because the Tao is the huge universal tree and we are a small part of that. Some of us are little roots, some are branches, some people are leaves. Some people are more rooted inside and some people are more focused outside but that doesn't mean that they're no good. They're all good in different ways.

When you say immortality, do you mean physical or spiritual?

For a Taoist, the main focus and achievement in life is to be able to become enlightened and to attain immortality. Immortality means you look at life as a whole thing. It doesn't matter how old you are. You can be one year old or a hundred and twenty three years old. However, immortality means once a person can focus their life into a center, from that center they are able to connect with the universal center. Discipline is the little bridge. It is the way you find the Tao.

Discipline meaning whatever practice you are doing?

Some people will take an airplane, some people will take a boat or a ship, some people will walk. Some people go fast, some people go slow. However you go to your destiny: through *tai ji quan,* through *qi gong,* through meditation, through various disciplines of *kung fu,* through laughing, through happiness; also with various expressions such as poetry, singing, chanting, or even talking to friends.

You come from a very strong lineage of teachers and practitioners. How important do you think that is for people in the West, where we don't really have that lineage connection? Like you said, we don't have that historical foundation.

We have a pure and great genealogy from China. We have two families. One is the Confucian family and the other is Chang Tao Ling family. I am the 64th generation master in that family. These are the two families that have lasted a long time. In the West, you don't have discipline. All the rivers flow to the ocean so we may be able to say that whoever studies Taoism is connected through this genealogy.

A spiritual connection.

Yes.

A lot of people think that Lao Tzu was the originator of Taoism but Taoism goes way back even before him.

Lao Tzu was the first scholar to describe Tao much more clearly and make the *Tao Te Ching* the wisest book in the world. This book really carries a lot of wisdom. It's a small book, but it's really great. That's the whole thing about Tao. A person can be really humble but he is still rich inside.

Taoism really goes all the way back to the cave times, when the ancestors were living inside the caves. They did practices with their hands to communicate with God. They didn't have writing then so the different formation of the fingers was like a language. The Chinese characters were invented on this idea of communication. The Chinese characters were not originally used among men. They were invented to use to communicate between human beings and God. So, what we call the Taoist magic fingers are a very important piece of history; of how early human beings were living in caves and using this kind of communication tool.

You can enjoy it as a religious practice. If you want to enjoy it on a scholarly basis then it is a very interesting philosophy. It is not about the idea that philosophical Taoism is better than religious Taoism. Some people feel more fulfilled if they can get into a religious practice. Some people will feel more comfortable if they think of it as beautiful poetry or a nice philosophy that they can practice. It is up to the individual.

So you feel that people can practice Taoism without necessarily being part of religious Taoism?

Yes, they can be either way. Some people are helped by having the faith and the prayers, so they are very deep into the religious practice. For their healing they need to get into that. Other people may feel the *Tao Te Ching* is so beautiful, it's a beautiful philosophy. It's enough to fulfill them and satisfy them. They can gain in wisdom to deal with life. Therefore, you don't really need to burn the incense and get deeply into the religious area.

People can practice qi gong and things like that without being religious.

Right. Various kinds of religious people practice *qi gong.*

From different religious backgrounds you mean?

Yes, I have Catholic priests, ministers, all kinds of people who are my students. The Chinese have a lot of traditions and you may call them all Taoists. Some of them came before Lao Tzu, before the Yellow Emperor even. As I mentioned before, it began in the caves, before written characters. Later on they used ropes and, as society became more complicated. they began to use characters. So it went from magic fingers to the rope to the characters.

It seems like one of the other great contributions that Taoism has made, especially to Western society, is Chinese medicine, which is something that you've been practicing for quite some time.

Yes, the Taoist healing arts, like the five elements, the foundation of *yin* and *yang*, the eight parameters, and the different ways to interpret the tongue—all came from the Taoist past. It's all Taoist curriculum. You can say that everybody who has studied Chinese medicine has studied part of the Taoist curriculum. For some people, they think that it is just a form of medical practice. You can find all of this information in the *Tao Tsang* (Taoist canon). It has all the herbal formulas, all the acupuncture points and all the meridians. This is all the Taoist curriculum.

Your school, unlike some Traditional Chinese Medicine schools in this country, really focuses on Taoist curriculum doesn't it?

Our curriculum is based on Taoist Medicine, a lot of *qi gong,* a lot of spiritual arts. You need to have a few schools who teach all these things because supposedly TCM schools are based on the idea of healing, a holistic approach, a natural way. The natural way is the Tao. They need more education in this way so that they don't go too far away from their root and become merely technicians. In healing people one needs sincerity and discipline. Practitioners need to do meditation and do some sort of movement, *tai ji quan* or *qi gong,* yoga or something.

I think that is one import part of Taoist teaching. It isn't just sitting and meditating, or studying books. You need to make it real in your body.

Right, you don't just say prayers. You need to be healthy.

Not all spiritual paths are like that. Some spiritual teachers say that the material plane is bad and we need to transcend it.

Taoism is totally different. We say that the body is your house, you have to keep it nice and clean. Your spirit lives inside and needs to be happy. You need to make the body nice and healthy, too. Without that you can not house the spirit, if you're floating someplace else.

Or if your qi is scattered or too weak.

Right, right. Actually people think that the body is not important and treat it like just some physical thing. That is wrong. Every particle inside carries a spirit. Every physical part cannot be separated from the spiritual. It's like the engine runs the car. If you don't have the car why do you need the engine?

You've found that Westerners are pretty open to these ideas and practices?

They're pretty open. The only problem is that they have a short interest. You must look into it seriously because it takes time from the television. They don't have time to focus on the internal. It's kind of sad because in the West, compared to many other countries, you have enough food, you have all these basic comforts, but you don't have enough discipline of the spiritual practices to make life more fulfilling.

If you're growing bonsai, you have a beautiful tree in a small bowl and you have to take care of it. You cannot just water it for a couple of days and look at it and then forget it for another month. Westerners' interest and focus is short. There is not enough long term discipline.

You've been going back to China a lot lately. Do you feel that Taoism is being revived in China?

We sponsored one of the major events with another temple. We get together with Taoists from many different mountains to have a ceremony all together under one roof. In 1994, there were two ceremonies, one in Beijing, at the White Cloud Temple, which was very big. Then there was one in Lung Hu Shan in October which went all the way to early November. It was a long festival. Almost all the masters were there.

So you feel confident that China will continue to be open about these things?

To tell the truth, the Chinese government has endorsed what these temples are doing. So this is a positive thing. All these Taoists came together under one roof. This is important, instead of you're the best, he's the best, and everybody else is no good. That's no good.

It's like when some people feel better about religious Taoism and some people feel better about philosophical Taoism and they each think their way is the best. How can you divide the water in the ocean?

To tell the truth, religious Taoism is just a tradition. Many people in China practice *tai ji* or something like that and you can say that this is a religious practice! Like worshipping the moon, or perhaps they look at it scientifically and say that the moon is affecting the water in the body. They say that they are not doing a traditional Taoist practice. Acupuncture, is based on the same idea. We tonify to promote the energy or you sedate to take away the excess. You can also say that this is a religious practice.

How is that?

You need to focus to build up this energy; it's a religious practice. You're using your mind and your spirit and then your physical act to achieve something. That is a religious practice. You do can meditation and say 'oh I'm not religious, I just meditate'. But do you meditate to achieve something? Or do you meditate to feel nothing? Are you trying to focus on something, to achieve good health? That's a religious practice.

This is why to promote Taoism people should not keep trying to separate the two approaches. This way we will heal each other. Not 'you wear robes and I wear short pants', you know?

It doesn't matter. When you go to some sort of dignified party you wear something better than shorts. If you go to the beach you wear something else. You don't need to wear a robe to go down to the beach.

In China today they're really working with qi gong in a scientific way to try and explain it.

Yes, the scientists explain *qi gong* in a scientific way. Religious people explain *qi gong* in a religious way. But it's the same form, the same thing. Just a different way to express it. It all has the same logic and value, otherwise it would have died out a long time ago.

Qi gong can be stretched to be very dramatic or it can be very simple. You just find the style that you feel comfortable with.

Is there anything you would want to say to Westerners who are perhaps new to Taoism, where do they start?

Never give up. Try a few breaths every morning. it will help you. Also a good place to start is by enjoying nature. That will get you into the Tao. Look for some books on Taoism at the library or bookstore or talk to a friend who is practicing *tai ji* or *qi gong*. Every morning close your eyes and put the tip of the tongue on the palate, then just breathe and swallow the saliva down to your tummy. Let all problems and turmoils diminish by exhaling them out.

5
Awakening the Healing Light of Tao
Mantak Chia

Mantak Chia was born to Chinese parents in Thailand in 1944. He has a background in traditional Taoist internal arts, as well as Western science and anatomy. He moved to New York in 1979 and began offering his unique blend of Taoist alchemical practices in a modern, scientific form. He now travels extensively and has centers and groups all over the world. In his workshops, he is dynamic and at ease with ancient Taoist alchemy as well as Western scientific principles. Dedicated to creating a form of Taoist inner alchemical practices that are applicable to modern day life, he has written over ten books, published by Healing Tao Books, Huntington, New York.

How did you begin the work you are doing?

I grew up in a country that was Buddhist and Moslem.

Which country was that?

Thailand. I was brought up in a Christian family. When I went to school, I had to study Buddhism. Later, on I went to Hong Kong to study Taoism.

One thing that makes you different from some of the other Taoist teachers is that you have taken the old teachings, and even some of the secret teachings, and put them in a modern, almost scientific framework for Westerners to understand. Is that something that you set out to do?

In the olden times, the Tao masters thought that they knew a lot, but it was in the olden way. In China, all the Tao masters had their own schools, or temples or monasteries. You had to spend your whole life learning their styles. They went into great details of philosophy and all kinds of singing and ritual. In that way, they had no time to study any modern technology or science. In fact, a lot of the old things that the Taoists discovered can be explained in one or two very simple, scientific ways.

The Chinese are very philosophical people. So when they

discover a truth, they like to go into a lot of thinking and dreaming and make it very complicated. I had a chance to study in a modern school. I spent two years in medical science, which is where I met my wife, Maneewan. She was teaching medical technology in a university hospital. I was also lucky to be able to study with a very traditional Tao master. In their Taoist system they have separated into ten different branches. So if you belong to one sect and you study under them, you have to follow their sect very strictly. If you try to come up with any other thing they don't want to accept that. But I studied with a master that did not belong to any sect. He lived in the mountains and was a real practitioner, not a monk or a Tao master who stayed in a temple.

He spent many years studying in a Tao temple and he was looking for the higher spiritual practice of the immortals. After spending many years in the Tao temple he felt that those people could not offer him anything else. He asked many other Tao masters who said that the only way that he could find anything higher than what he had already found was with the Tao masters high in the mountains. So he started to look for them.

Now those Tao masters in the mountains wanted a simple, effective and direct practice. When they went to the mountain they could not carry any ritual objects: no incense, no statue, no altar. They had to eliminate all these things and they had to go in the direct way. So they began to do away with all the ritual—chanting, incense, statues, gongs, music and things like that. When you don't depend on any outside thing, you must depend on yourself. When they began to depend on themselves, they discovered that the whole universe is inside us.

The whole practice evolved in a very simple way, but very effective and direct into the body. My master spent many years moving around, studying with various Tao masters. Finally, he found a master that would teach him just the pure and simple practice of yourself and the universe. That's how our practice came into being.

The microcosmic orbit?

The microcosmic orbit is just the beginning of everything.

One thing that I have always been curious about is that Taoism is actually the original philosophy of China. Why do you think that it has not survived in China?

You have to understand that China is so big. There are about seven or eight tribes of people in China. The Han is the majority. Over the years, because of the good life the people were leading, they began to get lazy and fat. The Mongolian people were cold and moving around, and were getting strong. They started to take over China. They knew the Tao masters and they wanted the Tao masters to help them control the people. The Tao masters didn't like this, so they started to run out into the mountains.

Then the *Ching* people came to control China. All of them wanted the Tao masters to help them control the people, so the Tao masters had to escape. They were put in jail or were killed. Then, when the Communists took over, they destroyed the temples and the Taoist communities. They even burned one thousand Taoist immortals. They took all these Tao masters who were sitting in a cave and burned them out. Now the real Taoist masters left are the ones that escaped China. In China itself there are not too many left.

I've heard that a lot of the people in China are practicing qi gong.

Now if you go to China, everybody says "This is the best *qi gong*, this is the right *qi gong*." If you go to another province they say, "This is the best *qi gong*, the right *qi gong*." After you travel for awhile you can get mixed up, because there is so much *qi gong*, and everybody says they are the best.

No matter what kind of *tai ji* or *qi gong* you do, the only question is can you get energy? *Qi gong* uses mind power to draw in the energy to transform the life force. Meditation and *tai ji* do this, too. Philosophy is important, but, you have to have energy and mind power to make it work. That is the problem with Americans. They understand the philosophy but they don't have the mind power, they don't have the *qi*, they don't have the steam, the gas to push the energy to move. Now when I teach I apply the philosophy to the practice so that you can use it.

The Taoists say that energetically, women are stronger than men.

Yes, energetically. Woman are stronger in the soft way, which lasts longer.

Do you have any basic message or philosophy that you would like to impart to people in the modern age that are being introduced to these Taoist concepts?

They must learn how to control their life force. They must learn how to transform the emotional energy in order to control their daily life. They must learn how to control their sexual energy, by controlling their ejaculation. Those are the things that Westerners need the most. They're very high in scientific technology and their life quality, which forms the outside, looks very good with big houses and automobiles and such, but on the inside they are very unhappy. They are very dissatisfied. They are too much outside of themselves. They have no control of their life force. They have no control of their emotions. They have no control of their sexual energy. So, in Taoism we offer a way to control your life force, how to control your sexual energy and your emotions.

So often we're controlled by our emotions.

People go and study a lot of mind control, a lot of psychology but they don't control their own lives. There is so much philosophy in Taoism, because Taoism does not come from Lao Tzu or Chuang Tzu alone. It comes from many millions of people. Everyone has their own way or concept about it. Myself, I like to go in the way of modern life. Some of the old teachings are too extreme. The concept of balancing is very important. Everything is balanced in nature. The idea is, how can you live in harmony with nature. To understand and live with nature, this part of Taoist teaching is very easy for people to accept.

You talk about sex as just a form of energy. Now a lot of people think of sexual energy as something that you can only do one thing with.

You can do healing with it.

That's a new concept to many people, that you can use it and you can move it around and use it for health and even wisdom.

The Taoist concept is that energy is everything, everything is energy. So if you look at it that way nothing can be lost. Sexuality is energy, emotions are energy, life force is energy. Anything you do on the planet can either be for harm or for benefit. It's all in how you use it.

This is how people can learn a way of life, learn the balancing of nature, and learn how to take care of themselves. They must learn how to take care of themselves first. Many people don't want to learn how to take care of themselves first. They want to begin by taking care of other people.

Do you have any specific vision for how your work can help the world today?

Yes, I feel that the Tao system is the universal spiritual soul essence. We are teaching the people how to have spiritual independence. The Tao system is very good at strengthening the body, strengthening the mind and strengthening the spirit. Throughout the history of China, we have had so many *qi gong* practices, and we have the *Tao Te Ching,* which is translated into many languages

The important thing is that what I learned is a whole system of mind, body and spirit leading to what we call the immortal Tao. Like the Christians, who believe in Jesus because he was an immortal. What they are doing is waiting for Jesus to come to make everyone immortal. In the Tao way you must work towards that yourself. It does not mean that you will not die, but that you are transforming your energy so that you can prepare yourself for the next life. That is the one major goal of the Tao that I learned from my master.

The basic goal of the Tao is to teach the people how to conserve and recycle energy so that they have more energy for healing, for happiness, and for helping other people. They must learn how to transform negative energy into positive energy. The most important part of a practice is not only the philosophy of the mind but to have the philosophy together with the practice. The sexual practice is the most needed in the West.

This culture is so sex-driven.

Yes, they drain themselves with it. They pursue sexual enjoyment, sexual orgasm, but they lose so much energy out of it, rather than gaining energy. The way of the Taoist sexual practice, which is one of the oldest sexual practices in the world— starting with the Yellow Emperor—teaches people how to have sex in the right way. How to enjoy sex as healing and spiritual growth and how to transform the sexual energy into the life force. This is different than being celibate and suppressing sex. If you have more energy, you can begin to convert all this energy into spiritual work.

One of the things that you have been identified with in a lot of people's minds is your work on sexual cultivation, but you also do a lot of work with transforming negative energy into positive.

One of the major practices in the Tao way to transform energy is the Inner Smile. In this practice, we learn to distinguish each emotion that is connected to each organ. For instance, hate and impatience are stored in the heart; fear is stored in the kidneys; anger, frustration, and jealousy are stored in the liver. If we dump the garbage together, such as worry from the spleen, we can create fear in the kidney which can create anger in the liver, which will eventually become hatred in the heart.

Now, in the West, people don't believe that emotions are connected to organs. In Taoism, we believe that if you can classify the emotions, you can then separate them. It's like you have left over food that you dump into your garbage can, then you change your oil and dump that in the same place, along with paper and pampers, all dumped into the same place. Then it becomes real garbage. Nobody wants to separate that garbage for you. Or else we give it to God, we ask for forgiveness and we dump our emotional garbage on God. Or we go to the priest and ask the priest for forgiveness, or we go to the psychologist and pay them money to handle our garbage.

In Taoism, we do not believe that someone else can handle your garbage for you. You have to handle your own garbage. You can practice the Inner Smile and the Six Healing Sounds using colors and the positive and negative emotional qualities. We believe that negative does not mean bad, it is just yin and yang. The yin is not bad and the yang is not good. The Way of Tao has discovered that negative does not mean it is evil or sinful. That is the first thing, the second thing is to learn how to classify them. Like putting the left-over food to compost, you put the oil change into a different container, you put the paper somewhere that you can recycle.

Taoism is very concerned about recycling and transforming the negative. With the Six Healing Sounds we use the color and the emotion. If you are not able to transform them, then you simply vent them down into the ground in a cloudy gray color so the mother earth can take them and transform them.

You learn how to smile to the heart and activate the love, you learn how to smile to each organ and begin to change one energy to another. You can change hatred into love and change anger into kindness.

The sexual practice is really only one small part of the Tao. We also have *Fusion I, II,* and *III* in which you learn how to take all the negative energy and use a formula to be able to have the negative energies counteract with each other. You use the fear to counteract the hate, the water goes against the fire. This way the two negatives will become transformed into a positive.

Such as in the five element system?

Yes, we call them the five forces of the universe. We use the five different forces of the universe to counteract each other or to give birth to each other.

As in the ko cycle, the control cycle?

Right. We have the controlling cycle or the creating cycle. When you do that you are able to transform the energy from the negative to the positive. In the West, it was once believed that negative energy should just be held in, but what happens is people get sick. Then people decided that you needed to express all emotions. Then everybody started dumping on each other. You dump on me, I dump on you. Society doesn't know what to do. The dumping doesn't work. The repression of emotions doesn't work. It's like dumping garbage in your bedroom. It doesn't work. Or you dump your garbage onto your neighbor. The only way is to compost them, recycle them, or transform them. We do that with our garbage all the time, but when it comes to our emotions, we don't know how to do that.

So we're transforming the negative by using the Healing Sounds and the Inner Smile, which are actually very simple practices.

Very simple and very powerful. People just need to learn the colors and emotions connected to each organ. For instance, with the heart they breathe in the red color, and when they smile to the heart, they are connecting to the red light. When they connect with the red light they can feel a lot of loving energy coming in. They have a lot of loving energy and the negative or hateful energy has less room to grow.

In Taoism, the important thing is to be able to take the problem into your own hands, but people don't want to take care of their own problems. They just want God to take care of their garbage, or God to forgive their sin.

Some people want to just go to a qi gong healer or doctor of Chinese medicine and let them do it.

Yes. At this time, twenty to thirty per cent of my students are acupuncturists.

The practice of the microcosmic orbit is very ancient, isn't it?

Yes, very ancient but I feel that I have improved it tremendously. Even in China they don't have what we have here now.

So in some ways, some of the qi gong that we are able to receive and work with in the West is superior to what you may find in China nowadays?

In China, they've been suppressed for nearly thirty years. They killed all the Tao masters so a lot of the pieces were lost. Nowadays, people take just one piece and make it so big.

Do you feel that your work is primarily in the West at this point?

Yes, I am coming from the tradition of inner alchemy. In the beginning of the inner alchemy tradition, they spent many years trying to find the pill of immortality. They tried for three thousand years but it never worked. Then, they began to discover that the changes had to come from the inside. The changes, themselves, are so simple. If someone makes you angry, and you can change that anger into kindness, you are an alchemist. If you are sexually aroused, you can become an alchemist. Recently in Time magazine they had an article called "Making Love Is Chemical Warfare". Everything is chemical inside the body.

It's too bad that they have to look at it as warfare.

Yes. Now in Taoist teaching, when you feel aroused, all the glands and hormones of the whole body combine and create a new energy. We don't really know what to call this new kind of energy so we call it the orgasm energy. That orgasm energy is the best combination of all the alchemy inside the body.

So it can be a very healing energy.

Right. If you ejaculate it out, though, it is lost. If you bring it up and circulate it you will have the alchemical changes and the most powerful energy in the world. That is what the monks and the nuns and the holy men discovered. In Taoism, we have the technology of how to do that. It does not have anything to do with any religious beliefs. It is the technology of the esoteric.

A lot of teachers today say that the age of being a monk or a recluse in the mountains and away from society, is over. We need to do our practice within society.

You cannot run away from society anymore, but people still try to do that. In Thailand, they say that for every one person who wants to be a monk a thousand people have to work for them. They have to build a ten million *bhat* temple for two or three monks to sit there and do nothing. I think the Taoist way is much more healthy for society. You stay home, you stay in society and you practice.

You obviously find that Westerners are very open to these kind of teachings.

Oh yes, more and more. Actually, now the biggest group of students are European. I spend four months a year in Europe.

I think the point you just made is a very important one: people can do Taoist practices without having to join a religion, or change their religious beliefs or give all their money to a guru or anything like that.

An important aspect of Tao is something we call spiritual independence. You give people the technology of how to go to heaven, if they want to. If you look carefully at celibacy, taking a vow and all that, it's good to take a vow and practice celibacy so that you can really do it. You become a monk and shave your head and put on a robe, you cannot have sex with anybody so you keep on working until one day you transform. But I tell you, out of one million monks, only one or two get it.

The work that you're doing in the West is in transforming the energy.

Transforming the emotional energy, and transforming the sexual energy. Transforming sexual energy is exactly like what the monk, nun, and holy man do. It's just that you can do it with having sex or by being celibate. People don't understand that.

A lot of priests in the West are celibate but they don't do any kind of cultivation and so prostate cancer is very prevalant among monks and priests.

Monks have the highest level of prostate cancer and nuns have the highest level of ovarian cancer.

That's because they don't do anything with their sexual energy. You can be celibate but it doesn't mean you're going to be healthy.

In Taoism we exercise the sexual organs. We have testicle breathing, power lock, big draw, how to breathe into the perineum, into the prostate gland, into the uterus. We have incredible success with people who have tumors and cysts there. We are very successful in helping women to shorten their menstruation.

In China, in the old days, this whole practice of sexual cultivation became very corrupted, with the ideas that you should not have sex with anyone that you really care about, or men having sex only with young women or with multiple partners so that it became almost like a sexual vampirism.

They were misusing it. In the way that I learned when you misuse it it is like a two-edged sword, it will cut you to pieces. When I teach I always say sex is like fire, when you put the fire in your stove it burns the food. If you put the fire in your house it will burn your house and kill people, but can you say that fire is bad?

How do you work with people to teach them how to use this energy in a morally appropriate way?

Sexual energy multiplies good morals. When people have so much love then sexual energy multiplies that love. One day I was watching CNN and I saw Mother Teresa being asked where did she get all the love to help people. She said, "I feel so much love in my heart, and suddenly I feel that the sexual energy rises up into my heart and I have so much love." That is what the Taoist discovered six thousand years ago. Love and sex have combined together. In Taoism we say that when water and fire are combined in the proper way we have steam. If the water is poured on the fire, it extinguishes the fire. If the fire is too hot, it burns up the water.

Sexual energy is the most important tool in any practice.
Without sexual energy transformation there are no holy men.
We say they are holy. Why? Because they work with sex. They
don't have sex with other people, they work with their own
sexual energy. In the Taoist tradition the holy men in the caves
are having self-intercourse, they are having sex with themselves. Later on, they learn how to have sex with God, which
is called bliss and ecstasy.

Like the practice of the golden embryo or the red baby?

Yes. If you want to have a baby, what do you do? You have to
have sex, right? If you want to give birth to yourself, have sex
with yourself. If you want to go to heaven you have to have
sex with the people who come from heaven!

I think, in the West, people are very very confused about sexuality.

The whole system is fed on sex. One secret is that all religions
are based on sex and magic. What do the Catholics do with
the young girls when they become nuns? They put a ring on
their finger and say now you are married to Jesus. Why do
they do that?

You can have human sex or you can have cellular inter-
course. The Bible says you must be born again. How can you
be born again? Nicodemus asked God, "How can I be born
again. Do you tell me to go into my mother's womb to come
out again?" Jesus said, "Truly, truly I tell you, you must be born
again." If you want to give birth to yourself, you have to have
sex with yourself. Taoism says you are a man and women within
yourself. So if you can harmonize the yin and yang, you will
be creating an embryo.

The thing that comes from heaven is the spirit or light. So
when you change yourself to be spirit or light you get married
to the spirit and you give birth to the new body, which we call
the true immortal. When you give birth that way you go to
heaven, because you give birth to a spiritual light that comes

from heaven.

What do you mean when you say you go to heaven?

It means whatever people think heaven is. You go to a place where we came from, the origin, or *wu chi*, or nothingness.

In China, a lot of the alchemical practices got very esoteric and only initiated people could understand them.

If I had only stayed in China, I wouldn't understand a lot. When I came to the West, there was so much happening here. One thing about America, it is the only place in the world where people can make money teaching the various systems. In China, you can not make money.

Don't you think that there may be people coming from China who don't necessarily know the real thing and are making money anyway?

Yes, but they won't last long. We have lot of *qi gong* teachers coming over here now to make money.

The nice thing about Taoist practices are that once you have learned them you can do them for yourself. You don't have to go to the doctor or the priest and have them do it for you.

What Jesus tried to teach is that your body is the temple of God. God tells you that you must build your own temple. You must become like a child. That is what all the Taoists are teaching, how to be a child, how to build your own temple.

6

The Tao Is Alive

Deng Ming-Dao

Deng Ming-Dao is the author of the immensely popular trilogy that begins with *The Wandering Taoist* and continues through *Seven Bamboo Tablets of the Cloudy Satchel* and *Gateway to a Vast World*. (published under one cover by Harper San Francisco and titled *Chronicles of Tao*). In it, he tells the story of the life and training of Kwan Saihung in the Taoist arts of *qi gong*, herbalism and the martial arts, beginning from when he is a young boy up through when he arrives in the United States and begins teaching here. It is a wonderful story, complete with exotic Taoist masters, detailed explanations of meditation and *qi gong* and lots of martial arts adventures. He is also the author of *Scholar Warrior* and *365 Tao*. He lives in San Francisco where he is a book designer.

Maybe we could talk a little about how you got connected to Saihung from your Wandering Taoist trilogy and how you decided to write his story.

Well, first of all, I met him when I was with two friends who were looking for a *tai ji* teacher. They said they had heard of this *tai ji* teacher named Mr. Kwan and were going to visit his class, and they asked if I wanted to come along. Thinking that he might not speak English, I decided to go along to help them translate. At that time, I was studying with another *tai ji* teacher so I was not really looking for anybody.

When we got there there, nobody was there and so we started practicing pushing hands, and this guy pops up from the bushes. My first impression of him then was that he looked like a biker, with big shoulders and a very wide face and his hair was kind of long. He was standing there in the bushes watching us and I was thinking, "Boy this guy is a real jerk." He was so obviously pugnacious.

Eventually the student contact that we had came up and said that the class was starting and when we went down, the guy from the bushes was leading the class! It turned out to be Mr. Kwan of course. When I went up to talk with him later—and it turned out by the way that he spoke very good English—I learned that he knew a lot of the things that I thought were legendary or lost or unknown in the U.S., and that made me excited. Unfortunately, I had another teacher and by Chinese etiquette I couldn't switch.

My two friends decided to join the class and Mr. Kwan said, "What about you?", and I said, "Well look, I have a teacher already," and he said, "Oh, that's okay. Don't come as a student. Just come as a friend." So that's how we got started together.

How we came to write the books was when Sifu and I were on our way to visit a yogi friend of his. Afterwards, we were driving away and he said, "You know, as great as this particular yogi is, I wish you had had the chance to meet some of the masters that I met. Some of those people were so powerful that when you sat next to them, you didn't even want to ask them a question. Or you would be standing there, and they would walk by you, and you would start weeping or laughing."

He said, "These are the people who are the true masters, and if the people in the United States knew what this type of master was they wouldn't fall prey to some of the charlatans who are out there." And I said "Well why don't you tell some of the stories of the people you met. Why don't we talk about your upbringing and so on."

Had you had experience in writing before then?

I had taken writing courses in school, but my training was all in fiction writing; which is the direction I'm moving back into.

The beauty of the books is that they are in story form. For many people it makes them even more accessible—the qi gong teachings and the meditation practices—to tell them in a story like that is very helpful.

To be honest with you, I find a lot of the scholarly works terribly boring, number one. And I have a special interest in this stuff! Number two, the thing that frustrates me so much about scholarly writing about *qi gong*, meditation, and so on, is that I never have the sense that they're written by a practitioner, by someone who has had the experience. I only have a sense that they're investigating scholarly sources and putting them together again.

I think people need to see that this stuff is not just scholarly, but that it is a way of life, and can fit organically into the way people live. That's part of the reason that I tried to write the books in that fashion.

The third part of the trilogy is pretty sad, because it takes him out of that beautiful mystical mountain top, and talks about the death of Taoism.

Well, of course my job was to write the story and not necessarily provide a happy ending. However, even though the Grand Master has pronounced the fact that Taoism is dead, I don't really think that is the case. Certainly, the way of life that the Grandmaster represents is dead, but so are a lot of other noble lifestyles that have gone by the wayside, not just in China, but in Europe, and on this continent as well. Yet we are still alive, and we are still people, we still have minds and hearts and spirits. The Tao is still alive. The Tao cannot be destroyed by anything humanity can do. So therefore, as long as the Tao exists, and as long as we have a spiritual side to ourselves, it is possible to get back in touch with that. It won't be the way they did it in ancient times. But it is still possible.

Taoism seems to have so much to offer the West. In this time where we have so many conflicting religions and philosophies, it is very very practical and basic and has practices and attitudes that people from any walk of life can use.

Yes, absolutely. I feel that Taoism has integrity. Taoism has tangibility, and the only reason why anybody would practice any aspect of Taoism is because it fits into their lives and provides results. That's the same for anything else. Nobody, including my teacher, is into practicing this stuff on faith alone. They're into it because it provides rewards, it provides a way of life, it provides an opening to something that is generally closed to people. So as long as it does that, then it's very relevant and very necessary for people to practice today.

And you feel that Taoism has a place in Western society?

No, I don't think Taoism has a place in any society. Taoism, as you know, is implicitly anti-social. It didn't really have a place in Chinese society. It was accepted in Chinese society, but as you know, for people to become Taoism renunciats was considered something shameful. Even my own teacher suffered rejection from his family when he decided to renounce the world. Therefore, Taoism in its pure spiritual sense, has no place in society. It has its more, shall we say, corrupt forms, where they engage in military strategy, or divination, or sorcery, and so on, where they will engage in political manipulation, but that is also Taoism. That is not the high spiritual part of Taoism that I believe needs to be represented.

A better way to put it, is that Taoism offers a very special reward to people in any society and that reward is still relevant today. Taoism is for those people that have seen the limitation of social mores, the limitations of social ambition, and want to find an alternative. Then Taoism is still relevant, and very important.

The practices of qi gong, tai ji quan and Chinese Medicine—which all have their roots in Taoist practice and philosophy—are three ways that people in this culture are beginning to get more and more interested in Taoism all the time.

That's true. Unfortunately, in my opinion, what happens is that people tend to see those practices in isolation. They tend to ascribe very magical results to something that is basic. It's like stretching, we know that a muscle gets more flexible because we stretch it. *Qi gong* should simply be seen as something that happens when the *qi* is circulated. That's it, when the *qi* circulates a certain way, then we get certain results . Some of those results are health to the organs or better blood circulation. Some of them border on what we would call mystical. They can all

What is not very well understood in the west is that things like *qi gong* and herbal medicine, diet, *tai ji* and so on are just part of a comprehensive system that can fit together and provide a continuum of understanding from the physical to the spiritual. That's what's missing.

I think that those people who look at Taoism and try to bring Taoism into a Western context are forever torn between the poles of the Western scientific method and the Chinese mystical method. While they try to get away from the esoterica of some parts of traditional Taoism, they then rush all the way over to the Western scientific view of *qi gong* or whatever, and in so doing, they miss out on the philosophy, the cultural understanding and the spiritual aspects.

After doing the Wandering Taoist trilogy you went in another direction with The Scholar Warrior, a book purely about the practice and then 365 Tao, which is pure philosophy.

Right, the whole idea of *365 Tao* was that if Taoism is so great, if Taoism is as universal as the masters tell us, then we should be able to discern it, and get in touch with it, each and every day, no matter where we live, no matter what's happening to us and so on. Everyday, on an ordinary level, there has to be some lesson about the Tao that we can learn. That's why I wrote *365 Tao*. I wrote one passage a day and the idea was, what happened to me today in an ordinary context, that taught me something about Taoism. So that's why the book is structured that way, in terms of daily meditation.

Well, it's really very nice. I hope you're not offended, but for me it's a great bathroom book.

Oh good. I don't feel that you need to have a long and obtuse dialogue in order to get a point across. I don't know if I'm just getting old or what, but I find myself getting less and less patient with long discourses.

Are you still involved with martial arts yourself?

Yes, I am. Let me tell you, learning martial arts is not magical. It doesn't mean that you can go out and knock some guy off his feet with one blow, even though that's what the teachers can do. The important things about martial arts are that it gives people discipline, it gives people focus, it gives people a sense of honor and strength that can't be overcome by adversity. That's the most important thing.

It's never enough, at least in the traditional Asian context, to just be good at one thing. You're supposed to be very good at what you do, but you're supposed to be very good at a lot of things.

Which is very different than this culture, where people are trained to do one thing well.

Right, and it's really a tragedy, because the one thing that they often learn to do well, which is usually a professional skill, does not necessarily have any ties to a philosophy, or spirituality, or health. For instance, I'm a designer. Let's say that I'm very good at design, and very good at manipulating computer programs and putting out products, and hitting my deadlines, and so forth. That doesn't necessarily do anything for me spiritually, or physically, or emotionally, or mentally. Then when I go home and have to deal with whatever is happening at home, or I go out to see my friends and so on, then I don't necessarily have any other insight from my profession. I'm still there with whatever I might have gotten from my school, or friends, or hearsay, or watching movies, or whatever the regular American sense of ethics is. It would be quite different in a traditional Asian context, where the insight that you receive from who you are is transferable to other aspects of your life. Any profession or any specialization can lead to deep insight and understanding into the most profound questions of life, whether you're a farmer, craftsman, potter, warrior, sage or ruler—any of those things, if they're done deeply enough, can lead you to enlightenment.

It is quite different from that in the United States today. But it's virtually impossible to ask someone to put themselves into that traditional situation, where you basically have to apprentice yourself to a master for decades. Your healing ability is a result not of technical knowledge, but a result of your entire being, your whole being is something that heals. When you reach that point in cultivation, it's extremely difficult and requires a fair bit of talent and quite a bit of time with a master.

So where are we? We have to applaud somebody who does that, if such a person indeed exists. We then have to look at the social requirements of trying to get people healed, trying to take care of people, trying to combat disease, and so on.

What we're talking about here is how people in the West can utilize these teachings, this philosophy, the practices, while not losing the real tradition.

And still have some integrity.

Exactly.

That's a tough deal, because apart from the kind of attitudes that you've been talking about with some of the other teachers, there are some contradictions between the Western outlook and the Eastern outlook. How to make it such that we can retain the integrity and usefulness without compromising it, that's a big challenge I think.

People in the West don't have a tradition of respect for the teacher, following rote memorization, getting up at five and practicing for two hours, following instructions that often don't mean anything to them, that kind of traditional Chinese teaching.

Right. Personally I've become wary of that kind of approach, because I think there's a lot of room for abuse. If you talk with someone who's been raised in an Asian family, I'm sure they can tell you plenty of abusive things their elder did or mistakes that were made. Although, supposedly, we've learned from masters and so on, the masters are still a product of their culture. I think there's still a lot of room for mistakes and abuses so I don't feel that the essence of Tao has to be transmitted in that way. Of course, you'll get a lot of arguments about that from a lot of teachers probably, including my own!

I remember that Yang Jwing Ming said that when he first came over to this country, he tried to be very traditional and the students wouldn't stay. Then he went to the opposite and became very friendly and familiar and they treated him like shit! So he had to find somewhere in between.

Yes, it's a very weird situation. There was a student assigned to me once. Even though he was older than I was, my master wanted me to teach him and I did insist that he call me Mr. Deng, not really because I cared about it, but because there has to be some respect and some distance. That respect, in my mind, is not for me as a person but it's for the tradition and for the role I'm playing. I don't take it to mean I'm so great or anything. For someone who's learning I would expect them to respect it (the tradition) and revere it as much as I do. Otherwise there's no use teaching them.

So I have no problems with Taoism coming to the West and people learning it in a somewhat non-traditional setting as long as the respect and the reverence and devotion are still there. And I don't think you have to be Chinese to have those qualities.

There's an interesting new book out called The Tao of Philosophy by Alan Watts which includes some of the talks he gave on Taoism. What I think is wonderful about it is that he talks a lot about really basic Taoist concepts but he very rarely uses Taoist terms. He's able to put it all into very ordinary language.

I'm really tending toward that myself! Not only as a way to get around that whole controversy of 'are we watering it down, should we be teaching it to the West?' and so on and so forth, but also because in this way it's much more accessible. There are a number of people who are actually going to want to go totally into the real traditional approach, but that number is very small. Yet, I think that people in general certainly need the benefit of these ideas and these concepts and they can start applying them right away. That doesn't mean that they are Taoist priests, that they are Taoist practitioners, but I don't see why they can't benefit from the kind of thinking and consideration that Taoists have given these ideas for centuries.

Have you done much teaching yourself?

No. I assisted my teacher in his classes for years. I assisted him in his seminars for many years and I had one student that he assigned me for a short time but other than that, I don't teach.

Is that because you don't have an interest in it?

No, well, partially that. And partially because, at least in our tradition, you don't teach until your master determines that you should. He's still out there teaching so why should I be teaching when he's still doing it?

So things are looking better for him than in the last book (Gateway to a Vast World)?

Yes, they're better than in the last book. I think my teacher is always searching for some sort of perfect situation, which is hard to find.

In this country.

In any country. I think one of the things that is never talked about in Taoism is that you become so sensitive, so interested in having a certain order in your life that's awfully hard to maintain in today's world. I think my teacher does experience some of those frustrations.

Hua Ching Ni mentions in one of his books that you can do practices and get so sensitive that it will be like torture to live in this modern world. That it is actually better to not try to attain those deep levels in this modern culture.

Until you can protect yourself in some sort of sanctuary. Otherwise, if you really were practicing, in a week you would be completely unfit for civilization. That's why I and some of my other classmates have had to pull back, because you have to work for a living and if you have a schedule of any sort; besides just what happens on the street, you just can't take it!

You come from a little bit of a different lineage than some other folks I have been speaking with.

My master does.

Yes, he comes from the Southern or the Western school?

Actually the *Hua Shan* calls itself the Western school. But even on *Hua Shan*, from what my master has told me, there were different sects. It was not completely homogeneous by any means. If you remember, in *Seven Bamboo Tablets of the Cloudy Satchel,* I alluded to some of the political things that happened on the mountain. That's precisely because there was not one unified school. In my master's case, he does come from a system that requires celibacy and it's not in favor of being a householder and so on.

A monastic kind of order.

Right. I'm not living that kind of life, though he is.

Does he feel that that is the way to do it?

It is for him.

Also then for his students?

Well, there are certain things that he won't teach to someone
unless they are celibate and that for years has been a big stum-
bling block for a lot of people. He knows that some people
aren't meant to be celibate so they shouldn't be. There are a
whole range of techniques that people who are not celibate
can still practice. But if you want some types of Taoist art you
have to be celibate. Unless you are that way he won't share
those techniques with you, unless you are initiated he won't
teach those kinds of things to you. That's just the way he is, he
is very pure in that sense.

*What about the monks and fellow students that he grew up with in
China, are they all gone now?*

The last time we talked about it, out of thirteen, there were
only five left alive. They're all older than he is. He said to me
that they themselves thought they were so pure and proud that
there is absolutely no chance of them passing on their Taoism.
Even in China there is no one that they have found to be ac-
ceptable as students.

Two of them did go to Vancouver for awhile. But they were
so proud and traditional they wouldn't cut their hair, they
wouldn't wear anything but their Taoist robes. They spoke a
dialect that nobody, even in Vancouver, could understand and
refused to try to learn how to do anything else. They had a

medical practice for a while and I think they taught some martial arts and finally, in disgust, they moved back to China to tell the Grand Master that there was no way that the West was going to get any of this stuff because there was no potential here at all.

You see, my master, as strict and tough as his students find him, in his mind, thinks he's being completely radical and modern because he cut his hair, he learned English, he learned different dialects of Chinese, he tries to make his teaching known to different people. He teaches women, which is not part of his sect. He teaches non-Chinese, which is not part of his sect. He travels around giving these seminars and classes which is also not part of his sect. So in his mind, even though to us we find him so utterly traditional and even sort of fiercely protective of his integrity, he is being extremely flexible and taking big chances of being thrown out of the sect for the kinds of things that he is doing.

In China, historically, there has been what has been called religious Taoism and the original philosophical Taoism of Lao Tzu and Chuang Tzu? Does you teacher came through that religious Taoism school?

I think in the West scholars have divided Taoism into a religious or monastic Taoism, philosophical Taoism and folk Taoism. In my master's case, he's definitely come through a monastic and religious sect.

Buddhism has become very popular in this country. There are a lot of different sects of Buddhism also and some of them are quite monastic and quite religious and a lot of Westerners are trying to live that lifestyle. It's interesting that the kind of Taoism that has become popular here is more through things like tai ji or qi gong but not the kind where you have to join an order of some kind. It really seems to have struck a chord in this country, this kind of non-religious Taoism.

Well, I think that religious Taoism is very hard for people to relate to. If you go to some of the temples in New York or Los Angeles, they are very hard to understand, because they don't emphasize the *qi gong*, the self cultivation, the philosophy and so on. Religious Taoism as it exists now, really has a very heavy emphasis on ritual, on chanting, on sort of devotional acts, social acts—marriages, funerals and so on. Very heavy emphasis on maintaining altars and things like that and I don't think the average Westerner is interested in that.

For example, I was with my teacher once when he went to see a priest because my teacher was always looking for the right place for himself and thought what better place to associate himself than with a temple. Interestingly enough, this temple had two huge murals going down each side of the hall and they were paintings of *Hua Shan*. This seemed like it would be a good fit and it was a very beautiful temple. But as they were talking, the guy sort of dismissed all the teachings that my teacher was interested in, the health aspects and so on. He said about martial arts, that 'sure you might need that if you're up in the mountains with the tigers but why do we need it down here?' He said *qi gong*, well, our belief is that when we chant, that is *qi gong*. When we do the devotions, that is our meditative act. We invite the gods into ourselves,' an almost shamanistic approach, and that is literally them inviting Tao into their bodies.

I think that's an illustration of how religious Taoism is currently practiced in most places, including Hong Kong and Taiwan. At present they really tend to content themselves with performing marriages and funerals and doing *feng shui* and a lot of divination. In many temples, you often have a choice of several different forms of divination. And that's how they pass on their philosophy.

You would go there with a question, say I'm troubled by this and the guy would say, don't ask me, ask the gods! You do the divination and that is how you get the philosophy, in their school anyway. They will say, okay, look, here's what the gods said and there you get your bit of philosophy and it's applied to your problem.

But the idea of saying 'okay, here you are, you may not have any particular problem but we're going to go through a long process of philosophical inquiry in order to make you into a special or different person,' I don't think that's really emphasized in the temples nowadays.

That's certainly very different than somebody doing their meditation or qi gong to cultivate themselves so that they can better understand and interact with the world and attain Tao.

Frankly, the teachers certainly don't make it any easier. My teacher's joke is, and it's not that much of a joke, is that in China the gates of the Buddhist temples are always open, they always welcome you in. In the Taoist temples, the gates are always locked. And once you get in they kick you out!

Traditional Taoists, let's face it, were extremely elitist. On the other hand, someone like my teacher sees no contradiction between that kind of belief and the very tough philosophical inquiry he's gone through. For him it's all part of Taoism. It's very hard to grasp that the same kind of Taoism that Lao Tzu talks about, is the very same kind of Taoism that my teacher connects in an unbroken line to the temple Taoism of today. For my teacher, that's all part of Taoism. It's very hard to resolve philosophicaly, why we are supposed to respect and accept that kind of devotion and the kind of very intellectual and philosophical inquires that Lao Tzu has come to stand for today. For my teacher, it's all part of the same thing. In spite of the kind of *qi gong* and philosophy that he has become known for through the books, he has a big altar and he has gods and is chanting every day and lighting incense and doing all these devotional acts and so on. So, it's one and the same for him and I think that people in the West are a little put off by that and find it very hard to understand as well.

Most of the people I talk to are drawn to Taoism, at least in the way that it is presented here in the West, because it is not another religion. It's not another New Age fad. There's nothing that you have to join. You don't have to wear a certain kind of hair style or color of clothing or even be a vegetarian. They like that. They like the feeling of spiritual freedom that's involved.

I think that people have come to distrust a lot of the established religions. They are looking for some sort of spiritual path that doesn't require an intermediary. Many of the priests of several different religions have, unfortunately, turned out to be abusive or corrupt. Then you ask yourself, 'I put my spiritual life in the hands of this person for fifty years?' So you say instead, 'I would rather have a direct connection please.' That's what Taoism offers. It does offer a lot of freedom. Unfortunately, with that freedom can come a lot of loneliness, a lot of difficulty, a lot of misunderstanding in that other people are not going to respect your path. It also takes a lot of determination.

My master always talked about priests that he saw in China that were euphemistically called "awaiting a visit from the gods". They felt that if they practiced with a great enough devotion all of heaven would open up to them. There are some very famous Taoist paintings of a meditator sitting there with the entire Taoist pantheon right in front of him. There were men who were eighty or ninety, and they were still awaiting a visit from the gods. He said that he was inspired by these people because, although the gods had not visited them yet, they still practiced with complete devotion.

Even if one adopts Taoist ideas and reads the *Tao Te Ching* and so on it doesn't mean that the fullness of the Taoist tradition is going to happen right away. If you have enough perseverance, in terms of understanding that this is a life long path, then you will "get a visit from the gods."

That's a good point. I think that self-responsibility is one of the key attitudes here and that's something that a lot of people have a problem with.

Yes, I don't think my master minds very much if Westerners pick up Taoism. I think he minds when they pick it up and then two years later they've lost interest and they've gone on to something else. I think that he feels that it's an insult to his tradition. Here is the one thing that has meant everything to him and for someone to throw it so casually aside is very disappointing to him.

In China it was thrown away because of repression and over here it's often thrown away because we have so much freedom.

That's right. Frankly, it doesn't matter what path you choose. It doesn't matter what religion you pick up. What matters is that it is appropriate for you and it resonates with you. I wouldn't advocate that everyone become a Taoist. It happens to work for me and it happens to work for me in a way that continually engenders more enthusiasm, more interest, more vistas to learn, more understanding that comes as the years go by. So for me it's a very valuable and wonderful life-long path.

A lot of people nowadays are getting into qi gong for health reasons. The practices themselves are often very simple but they take perseverance and dedication.

They do. They also require a teacher, because the deviation of half an inch or the wrong posture can send the *qi* off in a different direction. We have to be honest that although *qi gong* is very wonderful and very beneficial, it's not a panacea, it's not everything. As my teacher dryly observed, "if *qi gong* was really that great there would be no cancer in China!"

The other side of it is the morality part. I have heard of people in China who have become enormously powerful because of certain practices but their morality is wrong, like in The Seven Bamboo

Tablets of the Cloudy Satchel, where he has to go after his brother monk. People can get very powerful and it's easy to misuse the power.

Well, I think the Confucian influence on China is very strong. Even if you read Go Hong's writings, there is a continual emphasis on moral behavior. Doing good deeds is a prerequisite to immorality. However, what I understand from my teacher and what I've observed is that power is neutral. It has to do with the mind of the person and what they tend to use it for.

We know also that when one opens the lower centers and dwells on those centers then that power starts to tempt and one has to open the higher centers before one gains the spiritual insight to control the raw power that the low centers contain.

Yes, the lower center is the easiest to open, and Westerns really love to hang around in that center.

Sure. My teacher talks about many teachers that he has met that say, 'well I've got the root chakra open, the lower *dan tien* open, that's all I want to do.' Even when friends, associates or other masters offered to help them to go to other levels, they didn't want to. So it's not just a Western thing. My teacher saw many Chinese masters do that same thing.

Frankly, when you get to the higher centers, everything sort of withers away and you get very uninterested in things. When you're young or if you're really interested in physical powers and sexuality, all of a sudden you get to this state where sexuality drops away. That's very scary. Here you've defined yourself as a person by that power and then you have to ask yourself, do I really want to be that way? Also, if you have to work, and you have to do things, you open up these centers when you don't care about that stuff. How can you do a job that way? How can you even drive a car that way? So we're back to that same thing that we were talking about earlier. You can do that stuff when you have a sanctuary to protect you.

And, at the same time, you really have to ask yourself, are you ready to give up those feelings and energies that you for so long identified with?

The beauty of these practices and philosophy is that you can enter at any level and go to whatever level you want to. There are things that can be beneficial for you no matter what.

That's right. And you don't even necessarily have to do *qi gong* to be a Taoist. There were plenty of artists and poets, who through their art, which was so profound, their spiritually would rival a priest or a monk. What matters is that you live your life with integrity and depth and full investment and then the Tao will open to you. But if you want to just gloss over your life, and indulge in things and just go along with the crowd and never inquire into your own life then that's what you end up with.

I think we in the West tend to romanticize the East, just like they romanticize us. They think everyone here is rich and we do nothing but listen to rock and roll and watch TV and party. And we think everyone over there is a total sage and everyone is interested in spirituality. What drew me to Taoism is that it is a very earthy path. Just like China. Even the cities in China are very earthy compared to cities here!

It's very pragmatic. Yes, it's true, even in so-called wealthy circles it's astonishing how close to being an agrarian-based society they are. Even Beijing, it's amazing how completely surrounded it is by farmland. You go through the streets and there are piles higher than your head of cabbage and other vegetables.

To go back to your point about romanticizing: you also have to remember how over the centuries the Chinese have romanticized Taoism. If you even look at dishes in a Chinese restaurant, and you order broccoli, you've ordered a Jade Forest. You get a pile of shrimp and you're getting Dragons From the Sea. A plate of dumplings are Wonderful Pearls.

I think it's hard to separate out the kinds of techniques that we're learning in a supposedly scientific setting, like the way that *qi gong* is being taught today. We are finding that a lot of things have been exaggerated. Yet even when you try to strip away the romance, there is still something very magical about certain places in China. There's still something very wonderful about the techniques and so on. Only by experiencing it yourself can you come to some sort of evaluation of what is romantic and beautiful and, therefore, unreal and what's romantic and beautiful and therefore, very precious.

There is a part of Taoism and a part of China that is very precious and very beautiful once you get that for yourself. That also is part of it. Sure we want to talk about how Taoism works in the West, how it's good for health and spirituality. One thing that people don't talk about very much is that there is something about it that is so precious, so special, something to really love and treasure. Once that opens for you there's no doubt in your mind about it. There's no end to the road you walk when you are on your path.

That's something that I hope people will remember, that the path of Tao is a path that is very special and it is a living path that will provide for you forever once you get on it.

7

Keeper of the Tradition
Eva Wong

Eva Wong, Ph.D., is a practitioner of the Taoist arts and a member of the Fung Loy Kok Institute of Taoism in Denver. She is the translator of *Cultivating Stillness, Seven Taoist Masters* and *Lieh-Tzu: A Taoist Guide to Practical Living.* Obviously well trained in Taoist philosophy and practice Eva Wong has, in the tradition of ancient Taoists, opted for invisibility, hence the lovely picture of a crane rather than a photo.

When we first spoke, you mentioned that you come from a very traditional background in Taoism.

I think it has to do with being born into the culture. I'm Chinese, I was born and raised in Hong Kong. I was brought up in a fairly traditional manner in a Chinese culture, in which Taoism was a great influence. I grew up with it and it was natural to me.

You are involved in a monastic tradition now?

Yes.

That's something that I think a lot of people in the West don't know much about. Can you speak a little bit about what that's like?

Sure. There are basically two main traditions in the transmission of

Taoist teachings. One is called the lay transmission, which is essentially a non-monastic or non-sectarian type of teaching. There's also what is called the lineage transmission. The monastic transmission is one part of the lineage. Then there are other traditions, such as the priestly tradition, which is also a lineage transmission. Within the lineage transmission there are several branches. The monastic tradition comes from a historical development that occurred in China around the 8th to 11th century C.E. where people who studied and practiced the Taoist arts got together and decided that the best way to transmit the knowledge and preserve the tradition was to set up retreats. These are essentially hermitages in the mountains. They actually built them as learning institutes. By about the 11th century, the schools, seeing the need for discipline took a lot of the principles of behavior of the community life from Buddhism, which had its monasteries in China.

Which was called Chan Buddhism at that time?

Right. That's how our Taoist monastic traditions developed.

The institute that you're involved in, the Fong Loy Kok Temple in Colorado, was started in Hong Kong then?

That's right.

When was it transplanted over here?

In the nineteen sixties. That was when the teachers at the institute in Hong Kong came to North America and began teaching. Of course, because this is a different society than our traditional society in Hong Kong, the transmission of many of our courses were taught in a non-monastic setting. Eventually, what has happened in the transmission of the teachings is that we have made modifications so that there are multiple levels of involvement, and people can choose. It is not required that people become initiated in order to learn the Taoist knowledge.

So, do you feel that these practices and traditions do well when transplanted to the West?

I think they do. I think that any wisdom tradition does, because the wisdom itself is timeless and it's the application that we need to work with to make them relevant to the times that we are living in. I think that's really what makes these wisdom traditions great, they have been preserved throughout history, they are not frozen in time, so that the message is timeless.

I am a member of the Fong Loy Kok Temple. I am not an administrator, I don't like to do administrative work. I am one among many members. I also do a lot of research. Actually, I consider myself more a keeper of the tradition. I keep a tradition that is not only Taoist, but it goes even further back before Taoism actually became a word, or became a philosophy or a theory. Our origins go back way to the beginnings of our civilization.

That's an interesting point. A term like Taoism probably didn't come into use until Buddhism came into China, to be able to differentiate between Buddhism and the native Chinese tradition.

Well, there is a philosophy of the Tao which I think everybody agrees emerged with Lao Tzu. There were, in the time of the Spring and Autumn Period, which was around the 7th century B.C.E., many schools of philosophy, Taoism being one of them. Of course, Confucianism is the other one that's most well known. The business of the "isms" is really not Chinese. We don't have such an animal. It was really when the Western scholars began to study Chinese culture that there began to be these "isms" attatched to the knowledge. They gave the name Confucianism, they gave the name Taoism and they gave the name Legalism and such. We called them the yin yang school and we called them the Taoist schools, or the military strategic school and so on.

At one time, the term Huang Lao tradition was used for Taoism, was

it not?

Yes, the Huang Lao school was a term that was given to describe the Taoist school during about the 2nd century C.E.. It's a very interesting name because it's not used anymore, but in the 2nd century it was used because it was right there and then that Taoism became very closely associated with the health arts, and the medical sciences. Of course, we know that the Yellow Emperor (Huang Di) is really the ancestor of Chinese medicine and so when the two got associated together, the Tao and the medical arts, it became the Huang Lao (Lao Tzu) School. It was actually from then on that Taoism took on a very strong coloration, or interest in, the arts of longevity. Which we still have, as seen in the traditions of *qi gong* and the internal martial arts, and so on.

How much of Taoism today would be what you would call pure Taoism and how much of it is a sort of Taoist-Buddhist combination?

It's hard to tell, because any idea is never developed in isolation. It's influenced by other traditions and it has influenced other traditions. However, most Taoist practitioners would acknowledge that most Taoist traditions, although they were born from the original culture that is indigenous to China, have absorbed from a lot of other influences, of which Buddhism is probably one of the strongest. Hinduism is the second most important. As they say, you can't take something out of a cultural and historical flow, and Taoism was developed over several thousand years. In Taoism, we don't see truth as something that is frozen, that doesn't change. Truth and history interact. It changes with time and it changes people and people change it. So we recognize that Taoism has many influences, but we can also undo the strands and be able to identify that here was something that we took from Buddhism, here is something that came from yoga or Hinduism, here is something that is right from the root of the shamans of our ancient culture. We can identify those things.

On the other hand, would you be able to say, here's a way that we have influenced other cultures or other teachings?

That would be looking at other traditions. For example, Zen Buddhism is probably the most heavily influenced by Taoism, more than any form of Buddhism.

I think that is something a lot of people don't realize. They think that Zen Buddhism is either directly connected to Indian Buddhism or it's something that came right out of the Japanese culture.

Actually, Zen Buddhism itself is a very interesting phenomena, because it's Chinese and yet it's not Chinese. If we look at Mahayana Buddhism in India, there's no way that that kind of Buddhism can be accepted and make sense to Chinese people. They don't think that way. The Indians have a certain way of looking at the world. Chinese have a very different way of looking at the world. So, if you take one set of values and perspectives and try and put them on top of another world view it won't mesh. However, for Buddhism to be accepted in China it had to change. What happened to Buddhism was that it got influenced by Taoism, and because it was influenced by Taoism, it had to change its image and by changing its image it got accepted by the Chinese people.

I think that whole aspect of Zen Buddhism not relying on scriptures, the use of paradox in teachings, spontaneity, and emphasis on nature— all that's very Taoist. Then, when Chan Buddhism went to Japan it was taken up by the samurai class and now Zen Buddhism in Japan is very strict. There's a lot of just sitting, they don't do tai ji type of moving meditation. It seems like it got an almost fierce samurai overlay on top of it, instead of Taoism, which is the watercourse way.

Right. That's very interesting, because I have Japanese friends and I know people who practice Zen Buddhism and definitely when Chan Buddhism came to Japan and became Zen it took on the Japanese culture. Again, it's the same thing. Japanese culture and Chinese culture may have a lot of similarities, but we are very different. Before Zen Buddhism could be accepted and practiced in Japan it had to absorb the local influence, otherwise the Japanese would never accept it. At the time it was introduced to Japan, *bushido* was really the choice of living, it had to absorb that and because it did it was so successful in Japan.

I don't know a lot about Chan Buddhism, which is really Taoist Buddhism.

Which was really the forerunner of Zen. In fact the Chan Buddhism of China dwindled, once it got imported to Japan. In about the 12th or 13th century C.E. the political and social conditions in China were not very supportive of that kind of Buddhism. The kind of Buddhism that took its place, which is still the most popular kind of Buddhism in China, is the more devotional kind.

Why do you think it is that, even though China had Taoism, which to me is the most complete and integral tradition we can find, Buddhism became so popular?

There are a lot of theories. One of them is that there was a time in which the Emperors embraced Buddhism. It's a very interesting part of the history of China. When Buddhism became an influence in China was when China was split up into a lot of tribal kingdoms, around the 4th Century C.E., what we call the Northern and Southern dynasties. Basically, what happened was that the Han people, the long time descendents of the ancient Chinese people, lost it and were conquered by the tribes that lived along the border who were of Mongolian descent. The rulers then found themselves as a minority ruling over an extremely discontented and unwilling majority. So what they did was begin to adopt a form of what they called their own religion, which was Buddhism. They supported the monasteries in an attempt to fight the Taoist influence on the people, which was encouraging people to rebel against their foreign rulers. That was at a time when Buddhism was introduced to counterbalance Taoism. Then, as time went on Buddhism became established. It was absorbed into Chinese culture and simply became something that Chinese people accepted. Also, I think that as time went on, for the common person, there wasn't very much difference between Taoism and Buddhism. They looked to the traditions for spiritual guidance and to them it really didn't matter if it was Lao Tzu or Buddha.

Lao Tzu had been deified by that time anyway.

Right. It didn't really matter who it was that was the deity. What mattered was whether those religions or spiritual organizations supported their interests and helped them in their day to day spiritual needs.

The thing that's fascinating to me about Chinese culture is the Chinese ability to take on influences and even invasions and conquerors and somehow make them Chinese and make them a part of their culture.

China is like a vast ocean, everything just goes in and gets swallowed up.

Taoism is very concerned with self cultivation and not simply chanting for salvation. I wonder if, for a lot of people, that might be too much of a burden: self cultivation and self responsibility. As opposed to the idea that if you just chant Amida Buddha's name ten thousand times you'll go to heaven.

I think there's a point in this, as with all sacred traditions, what we call the level where the spiritual tradition is concerned with individual cultivation. It's hard, because you have to adopt a certain lifestyle, a certain attitude, to minimize desire and to work hard. You really have to spend a lot of time working on yourself. I think that is true of all the spiritual traditions, worldwide. As a result, the people who actually end up practicing a spiritual tradition in this way are few. However, the bulk of people, who will probably be content with having someone else do their work for them, are more attracted to the kind of practice that you can rely on a priest or a monk to hold you and take you through. If you pay certain respects you'll get certain rewards.

However, I think that what has happened in Taoism, as in other traditions, is that it is losing touch with what it really means to chant and to honor the sacred powers. When we honor the sacred powers, it's not asking them for a favor, it's honoring them for who they are and it is these powers that we acknowledge. They are there in the universe, and our chanting, our purification rites, and also our dancing, all are ways of honoring rather than worshipping.

You just mentioned chanting. Most people in this country are introduced to Taoism through Chinese medicine or something like tai ji or qi gong. Not many people know about chanting.

My particular lineage views chanting as a *qi gong* practice, because the sounds resonate within the body and enhance circulation. The five notes of the songs of the chants also resonate with the five internal organs. Also, on a more physical level, chanting actually loosens up blockages, because there are major acupuncture points in the area of the jaws. Also, the two meridians, the governing and functioning meridians, meet at the palate, in the mouth. A lot of the chanting is designed to connect those two meridians. Once we get into a more advanced level of chanting, it becomes a breathing exercise, a form of *qi gong*. The fast and the slow pace coincide with the hot and the slow fires, and this is really a way of transforming the internal.

What is it that you are actually chanting?

There are two basic categories of liturgies. Liturgies are sometimes encoded forms of instruction, like how to experience the spiritual world. It describes the internal environment. Everything is symbolically coded so that people who are informed in the internal understanding of these symbols know exactly what these instructions are. Chanting is a way for us to remind ourselves of the instructions in the form of mnemonics. If you chant frequently you end up memorizing the liturgy so that you always have the instructions with you.

Another kind of liturgy we do is purely sound. Mantra is probably the closest way you can describe it. That is where the Hindu influence comes in. We have Sanskrit sounds that we chant and those are also designed to vibrate inside the body and also facilitate the flow of internal energy.

What about the dancing you mentioned?

There are several forms of dancing. Many of the Taoist rituals have footwork associated with them. They can be performed outdoors or indoors. In our big sacred festivals the participants in the ceremony walk in a certain pattern that mimics the celestial movements of the stars, the sun, moon and so on. That is one form of dancing. Another form of dancing is what we call using the dance to induce a trance, so that the practitioner is taken to another world. In other words, the dance is a kind of shamanic journey to another realm to learn from the powers of that realm. There is also another form of dance that is more like the original shamanic dances where we take on the animal's spirit and honor it and become transformed together with the spirit of the animal, asking it to help us learn or to heal or to communicate.

There are lots of the things that most Western people don't know about. For a long time, the people who studied us were scholars, anthropologists and Smithsonian types. Also, the traditional Taoists in China don't really like to talk about their internal traditions with Westerners. There's always been a distrust of Westerners, because when the Westerners first came to China they came with guns and missionaries.

I see myself not so much as a Taoist, because to me that's just a label, but more as someone who keeps the tradition of my culture.

You do a lot of translating and writing don't you?

That's one way of preserving the culture. I believe that translations are a way to introduce a system of knowledge to another culture, so that there will be an understanding between cultures. If a wisdom tradition is truly universal then to me the best way to preserve it is to reveal it, not to keep it a secret. Which is something that a lot of the old teachers were concerned with, keeping it a secret. I think that for a long time the scholastic tradition had objectified things. As I was saying earlier, I don't really make a distinction between what's religion and what's philosophy. They're one wisdom tradition. As a matter of fact, in Chinese we don't have separate names for those things. The Western tendency is to want to compartmentalize all those things. Eastern people don't. That's why, when someone asks me if I'm religious, I don't know exactly what that means. I practice a cultural tradition and I try to also keep the ancient traditions of my people and make them available and known.

You come from Hong Kong, where Taoism has been able to be more out in the open than on mainland China.

That's right. It's very sad, because what China has done is really tried to disassociate itself from the source of wisdom that is the strength of its culture.

On one hand, there's a great fear that the culture as a whole will lose it. On the other hand, we do see signs of a small but steady rebirth of this tradition there now. Also, these traditions seem to be taking root and planting a lot of seeds in the West. At some point, China may have to look towards the West to regain some of its wisdom teachings.

I think that's very viable. It's something that we say in the Taoist tradition that there are two things that can destroy a tradition. One is you can crush it, which is what the communists tried to do. The other is that you can water it down, which is what some of the teachers have done in the Western world. And so, what we have to do now is strike a balance between keeping the traditional values and also making them accessible without watering them down.

I think that like Buddhism which got introduced to the West in the fifties and took about twenty years of transmission, it takes time to translate the scriptures of one religious tradition from one language to another and Buddhism certainly had all that time. Many of the Buddhist texts have been translated, but in Taoism we still don't have a lot of translations. What really surprises me, is that everybody tries to translate the *Tao Te Ching*, yet there are over three thousands books that are not translated.

The tricky part about religion in the West is that a lot of people view religion as going to church on Sunday and that's it. It's not something that you practice every day. So when people hear the word religion they are afraid that there's going to be a lot of ideology; a whole program that you have to buy into.

Religion only comes about when a spiritual tradition becomes organized. Religion is basically organized spiritual tradition. It's got a structure, it's got an administration, it's got a bureaucracy; for good or bad. It's got a whole standardized system. It's really a standardized spiritual tradition and in some ways that's good. It's a way of making it clear to everybody as to what they are studying and what they are practicing. On the other hand, it can be quite stifling, it can be lost in the mires of bureaucracy and administration. Especially in the Western tradition, it can sometimes turn vicious and mean. However, in China, one saving grace is that even when a spiritual tradition becomes a religion there's no such thing as heresy. There are no heretics, there is no persecution. I think that culturally, we have always been a very tolerant people. That's why, as you said early on, we have absorbed just about everything that has come in.

I've also heard it said that in the old days a Chinese person could, when doing business, be a Confucian, on holidays be a Buddhist, and when meditating be a Taoist, and that worked for them.

A lot of people in Hong Kong may have been converted to Christianity but they also respect a lot of the Buddhist and Taoist principles. They see nothing wrong in honoring their ancestors with incense and fruit and going to church at the same time.

For someone who is just approaching this tradition, what is the best way for them to get involved and find something that is going to be useful for them?

I think that if someone has the interest to learn more about Taoism, the best way is to not come in with any expectation. You need to listen, because once you have an idea or a preconceived notion of what you're looking for, then of course that's going to be the only thing you'll see and that will give a you a very one-sided approach. For example, if you think that Taoism is just purely *tai ji*, you will steer yourself to information of that particular interest and not anything else. Or if you feel that Taoism is simply Lao Tzu or the *Tao Te Ching*, that's the only book you will end up reading. So I would say that for a Westerner who wishes to be more familiar with the spiritual tradition of China, of which Taoism is the dominate one, simply be open and be prepared to be rattled. Expect things to be quite different from things you've seen before. You'll also be seeing things that could be familiar to you so don't come in with any preconceptions. Try to get a broad spectrum, because like feeling an elephant, its not just one aspect of Taoism that makes Taoism, but it is many practices. Spend all the time you want exploring.

When I talk to friends that are Westerners and they get really excited about one aspect of Taoism I say, wait, don't get into it just because this thing grabs you at the moment. Take the time to explore all the possibilities. Shop around, by all means. You don't have to get yourself initiated into a particular sect or spiritual tradition. You can try out all sorts of programs and find out which is the one that is the closest to your natural tendencies. Once you decide on one, you should stick with it, because learning an ancient tradition requires discipline and also a lot of hard work and commitment. So, when you have committed to one, stay with it and learn it the best you can, but also try to understand what the people, who were from the original culture had to go through when they learned it.

What do you think about people who just want to get involved with

qi gong, perhaps for health reasons, and are not interested in the chanting and the liturgy or even the deep spiritual aspects of the tradition?

I think that however deep one chooses to get involved with a spiritual tradition is fine. If a person is ill and wishes to get some healing out of the *qi gong* or *tai ji* or acupuncture, there's nothing wrong with that. There are some people who are more interested in the spiritual traditions, the chanting and the meditation. Certainly they can go to the appropriate sources for that information. Just because I practice and keep all the aspects of my culture, I don't ask that someone else does the same thing.

8

Living Your Tao

Chungliang Al Huang

Chungliang Al Huang is founder and president of the Living Tao Foundation and the Director of Lanting Institute in China. He is well-known all over the world for his exuberant energy in teaching the Tai Ji Way as well as being a personification of the principle of the living Tao. He is the author of many books, including *Embrace Tiger, Return to Mountain, Quantum Soup* and coauthor of *Mentoring: The Tao of Giving and Receiving Wisdom*. Trained in dance, music and calligraphy, Chungliang brings the living wisdom of Tao into the lives of his students in a joyous and practical way.

You are someone who has worked with the concept of bringing the ideas, the philosophy and the practice of tai ji to the West for many years.

Yes, I think I was enticed in the early sixties to start teaching at Esalen Institute, nearly thirty years ago. That's when I met Alan Watts. I was still an architect at that time, but because of the interest in my own background. I got sucked in. In fact *Embrace Tiger, Return to Mountain* was one of the first books on this subject that came out (1973). The book is now in nine translations. The last one that came out was in Greek. The Chinese version is now on the way, from Taiwan, actually.

I'm sure that you are aware that you are a fairly controversial figure in the world of tai ji. *Some of the older, traditional teachers consider what you do as being more dance than* tai ji.

I don't know whether you ever read one of my early articles called *The Tao of Movement for Dancers of Life*. I called it the *Watercourse Way Tai Ji*. I am very aware of the variations of the Ways. I am very careful not to officially call myself a *tai ji quan* teacher. I respect the tradition, I respect what other *tai ji* teachers are doing, and I don't want to create any controversy purposely. At the same time, my hope is to use my background and my understanding of the Tao to help *tai ji* practitioners have a little more creativity and a little more fun, which is something that is a lifetime's work. It is not something that you can learn in a three month's course, or even a five year apprenticeship.

In the West, we tend to look at the degree, at how you can accomplish something within a certain time frame, and then go to the right school, and get the right teacher. I've always been aware of that danger, especially when you teach *tai ji* in the West. We follow our own tradition here in the West. In the old days, you simply learned and kept learning, period. You accomplish what you accomplish. I always use the expression *tai ji* and not *tai ji quan* to make sure it distinguishes itself from the other *tai ji quan*, traditional form or style of learning.

Just like learning music — you can study Bach, but you also know that Bach is not the only composer. Bach is from the baroque period, which has a tradition. You love and respect Bach but you can also play other composers' music.

The same thing occurs in a dance background: you learn to be a fine dancer, not a *kind* of dancer. You can get stuck and get labeled as a ballet dancer, or a modern dancer, or a jazz dancer, and devote yourself to that tradition. My interest has always been to be a *tai ji* dancer. So, *tai ji quan* is one of the structures you can learn to do well. I respect tradition. I think that people who do one style of *tai ji quan* very well are wonderful. But my interest is to do many styles well and also to be able to make it *my own* style so that I can continue to be creative.

I remember a section that I really liked in one of your books. I think it was in **Embrace Tiger, Return to Mountain.** *You were giving a workshop and you were saying "This is not a military drill. We're not all lined up here to move in concise precision." The usual way* tai ji *is taught is that you follow the movements exactly as the teacher does them. What you are talking about is how can we have fun with this, and open ourselves and find our own movement within the form.*

Well, it's the same in all educational systems. Even in the Orient, in China, as a child I was exposed to people doing *tai ji* in the park, along the river or in the fields. As a child you look at nature, you observe how the first *tai ji* practitioners allowed nature to teach them.

Which is how it all got started.

Exactly. When you think of the so-called "original" *tai ji* master or the person who discovered how free, how beautiful, the simple movement of the body can be in relation to nature and you can feel wonderful with that connection, with that relationship with nature, and, you transcend your ego. You're not trying to manipulate and control what your body can do, but you're learning to allow the body to do movement naturally. This is how *tai ji* began.

You may remember in my *Beginner's* book, I talked about the *tai ji* mythology and I mentioned my own favorite *tai ji* lineage. I created a sort of parable about how once upon a time someplace, someone — it could be any culture — simply by meditating on nature with their body and realizing that they were a moving being, suddenly began to move as naturally, simply, joyously and spiritually as they could as a human being. And, that's how *tai ji* began.

That creative process is the true essence of *tai ji*. That is what my first book, *Embrace Tiger, Return to Mountain* is all about. And I want to explain to people how I feel the essence. It's wonderful to learn the choreography, to excel in the choreography, to be impressive by how well you can execute the movements. Sometimes the danger is that you can get trapped by how well you can do the movements, and the ego gets in. Then you are trying to be better than somebody else.

You may try to do it slower, have more control, or have more superficial looks instead of a pure experience. So I stay with creativity and refreshment of the practice. My own interest is to help people to share with them my own refreshment, how I regenerate, how I recreate my *tai ji* learning. I call it *The Tao of Movement*. And it's for anybody, for everybody of any age or condition. I think that's why *tai ji* is so popular, because there are no restrictions to age, to capabilities in your physical strength, or your abilities.

A lot of what tai ji is about is what's moving on the inside. The movement that you see on the outside is only what they call the tip of the iceberg. If the more subtle energy is not moving, then you can do the outside movements all your life and not get the full benefit.

I think that in the Western culture we tend to be impressionable. We are impressed by facility, we are youth-oriented as a society, and we like what is flashy and special. We tend to look at the surface rather than penetrate into the depth. *Tai ji* offers us the ability to observe the subtlety, the depth, and the richness which only comes from maturity, from age. When I was a younger teacher I was a very good mover,

I had a lot of good training. I started out with kung fu, and lots of dance. Muscularly, I was very impressive. But, I tried very much to restrain that impressive, external quality because unless you make the outside expression less facile, less sharp, you tend to show the glitter and you don't get to see what's really behind the movement. As I get older I realize that you are able to discover new levels of meaning as you have more depth in your own life.

I think you have done really well in encouraging the marriage of the East and the West. In the East, teaching is traditionally done in a rote manner, with little room for questions. In the West, on the other hand, we tend to go for that glitter. What you have done is to open up some of the traditions of the East in such a way that Westerners can move in them a little bit. I would think that would be useful for Chinese people as well.

Absolutely.

Are they open to this?

In my book, I talk about how when I was a young man in China, when I grew up with that tradition, it wasn't very special. I was more attracted to the glitter of the American Hollywood and the West, the newness and the fastness, and the kind of macho, Western, masculine energy, which is very attractive to an Oriental or Asian. I came here for that; I needed that balance. So, I often tell people how we Westerners have the classic *Journey to the East* (Herman Hesse) and in China we have our classic *Journey to the West* (Wu, Cheng-En). And even though that was a book about going to India to get the scriptures, when you think about how many of us Chinese and Japanese and other Asian people came to the West, it's because we needed that balance.

After I came to the West as a young man, as I matured as a young person, I realized that in order to be balanced I needed to re-establish my Chinese-ness. So, in a way my journey circled around and I realized my upbringing, my early training, was so meaningful and useful to my life in the West. Of course my timing was good. It was in the sixties. All that interest in *tai ji*, *I Ching*, Zen Buddhism, meant suddenly I was needed as a teacher.

Also, I was very lucky as a Chinese: I was a very good student of life and I found all my mentors. I was able to work with many teachers and mentors, who later became colleagues, and I started to hone myself and find a way to transmit what I knew. I think my *forte* and my good fortune is that I have learned the Western way of communication and am able to communicate what I know deeply within myself. I remember that in the early days many wonderful teachers came from Taiwan or from China. They were great teachers but they didn't know how to communicate. They were trying to teach Westerners the same way they taught the Chinese and it was very difficult. I remember Cheng Man-Ching in New York, on Canal street, telling me, "All these Americans want shorter forms. We can't keep them. All my American students ask me to simplify the form, to do a shorter version. So, if that's the way they want it, okay, I'll do it. But the real students will eventually find out that its too choppy, it's not organic."

So, I decided that instead of trying to teach the notes, I would teach improvisation. I also use the parallel of teaching piano: traditional teachers tend to teach the notes, you have to get all the notes right. 'If you practice long enough you get to Carnagie Hall.' At the same time though, you have all the people who are taking piano lessons, and only very few people continue to enjoy playing piano in their adult life. The same thing is true with *tai ji* students. We have so many people who take *tai ji* lessons and so few people stick with it, because it becomes boring or meaningless. Not only that, they get hurt. I have people coming to me who practice so rigidly, so consciously trying to hold positions, that they have knee problems.

Which is the antithesis of what you're supposed to be doing.

My early realization was that if I wanted to teach *tai ji* then I wanted to teach the joy of it, the freshness, the improvisation, the creativity. That's what the Empty Vessel is all about, because it keeps filling. You can empty it and keep filling it with new things. The empty cup you can fill with tea or soup. The empty flute you can play a melody on. All the musical instruments have that hollow space inside to reverberate. Now, we try and amplify everything to make it as big as possible. We want bigness and loudness and neglect the inner experience. *Tai ji* is an inner silence. We have to slow down in our very hectic lives.

What would you say to people who are not able to study with you personally, who are already practicing a form. How can they can apply what you teach to what they are doing?

Most people need a teacher, a mentor. The true mentor is the one who creates a guidance, and always pushes the student to be their own person. For instance, for many years in my network, which we call the *Living Tao Foundation,* I have resisted training 'teachers' of my style. Many people come with that wish and I say, "I can only train you, I can help you to be your own person." I do training programs to train the individual to be a living Tao person. You have to live in the Tao that is your own Tao. The living is your own personal living. You don't copy me, you don't try to copy a good example hoping you can superimpose another example onto your own life.

Many people want the safety and coziness of a big structure and umbrella, to hide or be safe under. The reason you want to call yourself a particular style of teacher is because you respect that style, you respect that lineage, which we all do. I always remind myself to repeat this, to pay respect to people who have a name that they call themselves because it shows respect for their lineage. I say I'm Chinese even though I'm an American citizen, I live in the West, and I teach in Europe. But basically, I owe my heritage to my Chinese origin. I am fortunate that none of my teachers want me to use their name to represent me. They all encourage me to be my own person. So, I encourage all my students to be their own person, to be their own very best *tai ji* students of life.

For people who are already practicing a certain form with a teacher, is there something that they might add to their practice?

When people come to my seminars or write to me I tell them, "Respect your own form. You have learned something wonderful. It's like a musician, you have learned a beautiful Bach or Mozart piece. Use it. Keep your repertoire. Meanwhile, keep learning how to play music better. Learn to improvise, learn how to be a good jazz musician." Some people say, "Well I can't improvise." There's no such thing as not being able to improvise.

Improvising with the form itself?

You must learn to disengage the form, disperse the form, take it apart and put it back together, like a puzzle. It's like doing a picture puzzle. You put it all together again but you don't keep it there, or you'd lose all the fun. You break the puzzle apart and then you put it back together.Not everyone does the puzzle in exactly the same way. We can't step into the same water twice, which means every time you practice your form you are starting a new improvisation. Eventually you will re-create that form in a new way and you will look at the form differently.

In jazz music, you usually have to have your 'chops' down before you are able to improvise intelligently. Do you feel that the beginning student should learn the form as taught before they begin improvising?

Certain people need that structure before they can be set free. Certain people can be very free and eventually learn the structure. I think you need to know who you are. My own personality is such that I would be totally frustrated and I would rebel against structure. I also love the form. At the same time I feel that if you get stuck in any one style you become the prisoner of your own rigidity. So my learning has been to encourage people to tap into their own creative ability, and to say that you are already a *tai ji* dancer. It's great also to learn a form. More important than anything, you want to honor your teachers with your own freedom, your own spontaneity. Every good teacher will agree with me that no one wants to make you rigid.

Then you lose the softness of the form.

Yes, and it also takes disciples to create gurus. Disciples need gurus as gurus need disciples. There are good gurus, wonderful gurus, who are mentors and teachers who create empty space for the students. There are wonderful students who are so humble, and at the same time have enough self esteem and sense of self worth, to know they don't belong to the guru.

My contribution to the *tai ji* world, to the Tao world, is the *living* part of it. It is the creative trust in oneself. At the same time, I have respect for the traditional teachers, for the 'masters' of lineage, because that is something we need also. We need the old wisdom, we need lineage to transmit the old wisdom. But we do not want to be slaves of ancient ways that are not contemporary enough for us to live here in today's life. We have to live in the now. We have to bring the past into the future through living now.

This is why your magazine is interesting to me, because you are talking about contemporary Taoism. When I gave a talk at the World Religion Congress in Chicago recently, I said that I represent Tao without "ism". With all respect for the "ism" we need to label, we need to call it Taoism to give it a framework. But we know that Tao defies "ism". If Tao gets stuck with "ism" then it would be separated from the rest of life. Tao may be the most open, philosophical, religious form that there is. That's parallel to my *tai ji* view, which is to create *tai ji* learning without the rigidity of structure, with all the respect for the structure. Nature is the same thing. We know there are forces there. But nature tells us that every force is different. We have a calendar, we have hours on our watch, but we know it's only a structure to help us to find the real time and the real seasonal cycle. If we get stuck with the first day of spring, or we get stuck with twelve o'clock sharp, (without spontaneity), we lose our Tao.

How does one start to improvise without losing the internal movement?

You need to learn that nature is bigger than you are. Your own body is more wise than your intellectual thinking of what your body can do. In the West, we tend to be mechanical because we come from the lineage of logic and rationalization and the Cartesian idea that the universe is mechanical. The balance to that mentality is that nature has a bigger mind than our human limitations. I think if we meditate on the body — and this is what the *tai ji* dance is all about, transcending your ego control of the body — then the body teaches you that there is more understanding there than you think.

Now, the difference between a child squiggling a line totally spontaneously and a Picasso or a Paul Klee, is that a child is spontaneous and once in a while may hit upon a spontaneity comparable to nature. But the minute you become self-conscious you can't do that any more. Then you have to really cultivate yourself to become a true artist. Like Picasso, finally in his old age, could just make a simple line; or Matissse could just use a cut-out and we know it's wonderful because they have accumulated all that experience, plus, they are great artists because they know how to sustain spontaneity. Maybe a better way to put it is that they learn how to never lose spontaneity. You can't hold on to spontaneity! You cannot pretend to be spontaneous. If you keep that open space, then you realize that something fresh, something childlike will always come through. And that you can trust — because as a child you knew, you were closer to nature than you are now with an adult ego.

Every morning when you wake up and you discover your body can move, what a miracle! If you can use that same spirit when you practice your *tai ji*, you will become so happy with the simple *tai ji* movements, instead of going through the set and saying "Well I've done so many moves and I've fulfilled my requirement." With that attitude there is the danger that eventually you will get bored with it, and will find something else more interesting to take the place of this boring routine.

Which may be why so many people don't stick with it.

Exactly. This is why they quit. It doesn't fulfill their spiritual and emotional and creative needs anymore. My job has always been to be sure that everybody still gets excited with their very first movement. When you open your arms you have to say, "Wow." You have to take a good look at your new beginning. I find that as long as I keep my own freshness when I teach, then I can always create a new class. My most advanced students are best beginners.

With that Beginners Mind.

Yes. That is why they come to study. They need to refresh themselves, they need to get excited with their lives and with their movements all over again.

I think a real teacher is someone who embodies whatever it is that they are teaching.

Well, it's life; it's living your Tao, Tao for every day living. You have to live it; Tao is not something you acquire. You do not get a degree to become a Taoist. You do not become a first or second degree *tai ji* dancer. You are not there to prove your external worth or your clout over other people. It's not one-upmanship. You're competing with yourself in your own practice.

Although they do have tournaments and people win trophies in their form.

In my humble opinion that is to fulfill the human need. In Japan you have degrees for your belt. In China we never had that system.

Even in kung fu?

No, hardly ever. The basic truth is that the minute you see the person walk into the room you know how good he is. Every once in a while I have to show people. Just move your arms up. I see your first move, you don't need to go through your hundred and eight moves for you to show me how well you can move. All your have to do is make two gestures and I can tell. Just because you wear a badge saying you have done five years of training, and you got your certificate, it doesn't mean you're any better. Human beings need this assurance. Now and then I use my titles just to impress people because those people need to be impressed. I don't take it seriously though. But, if you get caught up with your trophies, then you are in trouble.

I thought it was very interesting that Alan Watts, who wrote for many years about Buddhism, and was very instrumental in bringing Buddhism to the West and who was a very great intellectual— towards the end of his life he wrote a book, The Watercourse Way, about Taoism, in a very un-intellectual and very playful way.

I was very fortunate in that he was one of my mentor-teacher-friends. He taught me a great deal. He kept telling me that I taught him much, also. I think it was a mutual give and take. He came from the rigid West, in England. There was a spontaneous *tai ji* dancer trying to get out. He became known for his intellect. But he used to say to me, "Don't you dare improve your English, because then you will be as trapped as I am with my language facility."

We were a good combination because he said, " You can show people how to experience what we talk about." He knew that he could talk about it intellectually, but he loved experience. He was like a child experiencing with me the *tai ji* movements. He loved rituals. The reason he loved Zen so much is because he loved the Zen rituals. He loved Tao so much because he loved the *tai ji* idea. He started to learn *tai ji* with me and he learned how to dance. In his early life he couldn't dance. Even though the book was unfinished in many ways it was the way it ought to be, like an unfinished book of Tao should be, to leave some open space for people to fill in.

I think many people now, after a retrospect of twenty years, probably regard that book as his most spontaneous, his most right-on book. It was his most experiential book, the most lived, and spontaneous.

We are interested in contemporary Taoism because we wish to bring this ancient heritage into every day lives, and help to make this very troubled world a more humane place to live in. It is a legacy we hope to leave for the world. The current interest in *qi gong* and *tai ji* is obvious, because we are concerned about health and well being. Often people with this practical incentive find their way into the learning. Most of them are so out of touch with their bodies. They wish to get back in shape, and honor their bodies that house the mind and the spirit. When they have made this integration, they begin to live again, more fully.

That seems to be an important way of entry for a lot of people nowadays.

Yes, when people lose their health, their bodies are not functioning well. They are eager to restore their wellness by going into therapy or enter into what I call the transpersonal *tai ji*. You learn to get beyond this little needy person, me. This healing aspect of the Living Tao is closely linked to health and well being, through creativity, music and dance; the arts in general.

This is the essence of *tai ji*. You get out there in the morning and you do personal therapy. You attune yourself and you get yourself balanced; body, mind and soul. You also live in the practical world. In business, you are dealing with competition, achievement and performance; you learn to excel in this world to succeed. You also need to learn to keep your life in balance.

I was recently interviewed by the Ross Group in Boston, a very innovative business consulting management firm. They are featuring me in their fall newsletter about how to use Eastern practice to produce performance breakthroughs within business companies world wide.

My interest is more than just to create a sanctuary, a place for people to get away from work in order to find solace and balance. You can always run away to temples, zendos, or to a *tai ji* seminar; or go all the way to a retreat in the Orient. It is much more meaningful and real to learn not to separate your learning from your daily life right here at home. We must bring the Tao essence into our practical living.

What would be the Taoist approach to competition then?

All my books are in some ways dealing with that. Especially in my book with Jerry Lynch, *Thinking Body Dancing Mind.* We mixed metaphors to shift people's consciousness, using the Tao approach to soften the hard edges of winning, competition and performance. One of my dear friends, David Brower, whom I respect and admire deeply, just wrote a book entitled, *Let the Mountains Speak, Let the Rivers Run*— a very Taoist title indeed. David and I both support the Windstar foundation, co-founded by John Denver and Tom Crum. For 15 years, I have been involved in helping the wonderful work there on eco-logical re-education. In the last ten years, we also participated in their annual symposium called *Choices for the Future* in the Music Tent in Aspen, Colorado. My contribution is to bring *tai ji* and the Living Tao essence to the conference for the multi-cultural partici-pants, who have interdisciplinary interests and expertise.

To get people out of their heads.

Exactly. I tell them to practice *tai ji* to understand nature, to not only talk about ecology and environmental awareness, but to embody it and use the learning in their lives. Another kindred friend I collabo-rate with is Fritjof Capra who wrote the classic, *The Tao of Physics*. His current focus is on eco-literacy. He and I have been giving semi-nars together for several years now at Esalen Institute. This year we call it *The Patterns of Life*. He uses his scientific point of view called Systems Theory. I use the Taoist concept about the Watercourse Way, with my brush calligraphy to show the patterns of energy and the flow of *qi*. So here we enter into ecology with Tao. Taking small 'danc-ing' steps toward an ecology of mind, body, and spirit. The new buzz word in science now is the Chaos Theory.

Taoists came up with the original chaos theory, didn't they?

In Chinese, we call it *Hun Tun*—the formless form, or the sensitive chaos. Marie-Louise von Franz and I used *Hun Tun* to talk with the Jungian psychologists in Zurich. Tao is a living science, and science is now embracing the Tao. My work is to help make Tao accessible and connect it to people who are scientific, or need scientific proofs to enter into the Tao.

I think Joseph Needham showed that in his work years ago.

Yes, he was the forerunner. He and his collaborators began mostly as scientists, and ended up as Taoists. They studied Chinese civilization, and realized that the Chinese philosophy, especially Taoism, played a big part in the wise containment of China's formidable early scientific achievements. Contemporary Taoism embraces the world culture. Tao and the spiritual traditions of the world are actually very compatible with the recent and future advancement of science.

And Tao as religion?

Tao is the universal philosophy of living. If we wish to think of Tao as religion, it is a Religion with a big 'R', with no separate denominations. We may look at the differences, but focus on the sameness. My favorite translation of the first line of the *Tao Te Ching* is: 'The Tao that can be 'ismed' is not the Tao.' The Tao student of Life who becomes an 'ist' misses a big chunk of Tao and becomes a small 't' taoist. The Tao cannot be 'ismed'. If we only see the term Taoism as a concept, it can be very confining. We need to open it up, and allow ourselves to grow in and fulfil Tao.

Let's be sure we open Tao to the education system. We need to learn how to create a learning environment, without hierarchy, without the teacher on the podium always looking down at the students. The true mentor does not have to lead all the time.

I have found through *tai ji* movements and through the living body, a totally different way of learning. In Asia, where my roots are, they have a very good early childhood education program. Small children are very much nurtured, the way children are lovingly cultivated in the Children's Palaces. Of course, once they go to school, like in all schools wherever you are, they lose their innocence. My work is to help sustain this precious childlike nature. Childlikeness is the essence of the Tao. The *Tao Te Ching* asks us: "Can you be like an infant? Can you be the eternal child?" Can you sustain this sense of wonder in daily living?

Become as a child to enter the kingdom.

Yes. You can easily become a child again through movement, dance and music. I use a great deal of creative imagination to help the individual sustain and rediscover their childlikeness. These are some of the essential tools in mentoring. We must re-instill mentoring in education; we need to sustain and nurture the child-nature in learning, no matter how grownup we have become.

I would like to tell you about Yehudi Menuhin's work with children in music. As a child prodigy he never really had a childhood. So he established a school in England where I was a guest teacher a few times. He transformed a country estate into a warm and loving learning environment. He invites prodigious children there to give them the best musical training available; and he also provides them with a home and family life so they can continue to grow as healthy children, while they practice diligently in their crafts. He is now establishing an international association to help and nurture music teachers, providing them with continuing creativity and growth, including my support with the *tai ji* learning. It is a collaboration with the European Music Council and UNESCO.

Would you discuss the difference between a mentor and a master?

Master is a term which describes an individual who has mastery over whatever he is doing. A master may or may not be a good mentor. He may be a master of his art, but until he learns to become a master teacher as well, who can share his learning on equal terms with his students, he has yet to become a mentor.

So a master is not necessarily a mentor.

Many teachers are not necessarily good mentors. They may be able to teach what they know, but they are not very good at learning from what they teach. To be a mentor you need to first be a good student and teach your learning at the same time.

How do you define mentor then?

A mentor, to me, is someone who can be a leader and a follower at the same time. You need to have as much enthusiasm to learn from your students as you do to teach them. If you just teach, it's only half of the *yin/yang tai ji* circle. The same goes with the master. Being a master only implies that you are complete within yourself, that you have achieved a high standard in your own learning and discipline, but that does not necessarily mean you know how to transmit it to other people, or if you even have the goodwill to transmit your mastery to others.

Can one be a mentor without being a master?

Yes. You can be a mentor if you have a great desire and passion for learning. The most important gift that you can give to your students is to share the passion of this learning. You learn together. This passion to learn is the Tao. Knowledge is something limitless; wisdom is something you feel in your heart and in your gut. But knowledge can be essentially superficial because it just keeps on accumulating, which clutters and confuses. Wisdom is knowledge digested and crystalized, ready to be transmitted spontaneously. You may be able to accumulate practical knowledge to teach, but you must also have inner wisdom to be a good mentor.

How do you mentor then?

The subtitle of our mentoring book is *The Tao of Giving and Receiving Wisdom*. Of course you learn to give wisdom, but it is more important to learn to receive. Wisdom happens when the giving and taking take place in the *tai ji* dance. In this *tai ji* dance between learning partners, we call *Tui Shou*, the joining hands practice. It is a subtle work. It is sometimes called 'push hands'. It has a wonderful image in which you co-create an open center to share the mentoring process. We also call it bridging hands or sticking hands. In Chinese *tui* literally means push, but in *tui shou* you also gather. You push-give, but you immediately gather and invite back.

That takes it out of the martial arts realm, too, of trying to knock someone over.

Exactly. *Tai ji* is a dance for yourself, and with others. The reading line of our mentoring book is *Cultivate Dynamic Relationships in All Arenas of Life*. We wish to expand the mentoring beyond the obvious relationships between teacher and student, parent and child, employer and employee; to all possible inter-relationships for all people. When you mentor, you create a dynamism instead of a static hierarchy or opposition. When it is dynamic you begin to feel the flow, you start to dance.

Tao is openness, Tao is a way to let things live and be. Again, we go back to living our Tao. Otherwise, Tao is merely a nice idea, a dry and sterile concept.

It strikes me, from some of the things that you have been saying, that there are many people in the world who are Taoists who have never heard of Lao Tzu or even the term Tao.

We need to let people know that and help them enter into the essence of who they are. To help them not only balance and integrate their own lives and living their own Tao, but also realize that there are many people like themselves who are already doing the work and already making the world a much more balanced place to live in. We have here the East/West polarity between two very different philosophies and ways of looking at life. We may think we are aware of this intellectually, but we still need to learn to experience the differences, and at the same time find the unity and harmony in diversity.

Another person I would like to mention is Brother David Steindl-Rast, a Benedictine monk who is a true mentor. He and I collaborate on an annual seminar at Esalen called *Body Poetry, East and West*. We began using the Chinese concepts of the Five Elements as metaphors, then the *I Ching* trigrams and hexagrams. He brings the Western spiritual tradition and I bring the Asian. We use poetry to explain and explore this wonderful connection between East and West, through the metaphoric mind and body, in spiritual dimensions. He is a monk, psychologist, philosopher and a Taoist brother to me.

Look at what Thomas Merton did with Chuang Tzu.

Yes, Brother David is, in another way, a catalyst like Merton. He is just as thoughtful. Another kindred soul is David Darling, the virtuoso cellist and brilliant musician-educator. David founded a network called *Music for People*. He encourages and brings out the long lost musician in everyone. We teach together every New Year at Esalen, *The Tao of Music and Movement Meditation*. This January we call it *Tao Mentoring in Music and Tai Ji*. He is another true Taoist with the big 'T'. He uses Bach and Jazz and delightful improvisation skills to help inspire thousands of people to rediscover the joy of music. He incorporates all the *tai ji* techniques we share, with the Five Elements and *I Ching* metaphors for play, dance and music. We have shared some wonderful concerts and teaching throughout the years.

You definitely lead an interesting life, don't you?

I have been blessed. We say in China, 'when the student is ready, the teacher appears'. I have always been ready. My mentors: Alan Watts, Gregory Bateson, John Blofeld, Lama Anagarika Govinda, Laura Huxley, Han Suyin, Jean Erdman and Joseph Campbell appeared. I count my blessings and I never take my good fortune for granted. Happiness is based on your deep understanding and appreciation of your good fortune. If you are grateful for your life, then you are a happy person. I am very grateful for my good life!

We learn to live our Tao. The world we live in is a Living Tao world. Tao is universal and spiritual in a global sense. Tao is for everyone in all cultures to enter and partake. Many sinologists or scholars tend to concentrate on specific aspects of the Asian philosophies. I am a generalist, interested in multi-dimensional, interdisciplinary studies. I am not a specialist; I wish to be more inclusive, instead of exclusive. I am interested in inviting people from all walks of life, all cultural backgrounds to enter into the Tao in everyday living .

And, through mentoring and maturity, we enter into Saging, a word I made up for conscious 'Tao' aging. I am reaching a time in my life when I appreciate and value my insight-full and meaning-full aging process. Surely the moment you are born you are already aging. Until you reach midlife, aging only means growth. After midlife we need to learn how to Sage, instead of age. As a youth, growing older is an exciting process. After midlife, it's a different story. Most people are threatened and fearful of their physical decline. In Saging, first you need to take care of your bodily health and spiritual well being. That's the obvious thing to do. Then you realize you are ready to enter mentoring, learning the Tao of giving and receiving wisdom. We sometime joke about older folks entering into their second child-hood. This tapping into our childlikeness is a major step in Saging. We learn to honor our age and experience, to entertain the ability to be a child again and in our openness rediscover our sense of wonder and awe.

I look forward to this well-earned mentoring leverage, to use my experience and self-esteemed integrity to share with people from all walks of life. Saging is the awareness that in the center of all your accumulated knowledge, there is indeed some wisdom and you have earned the respect and advantage to share this wisdom freely. As a person living his Tao, I need to constantly re-assess my true wisdom, not just the accumulation of knowing. The Saging process is not only important for middle-aged people who are facing this choice of ag-ing gracefully, it is also vital for young people, who are already ob-serving their grandparents' and parents' aging. If you are sensitive and alert, and thinking with a Dancing Mind, you can learn a great deal about saging while you are still young. You can see some people saging very gracefully, and others aging miserably. So you can learn and become wiser, sooner.

Warning: The minute you think you are wise you may stop learn-ing. If you are happy with the little wisdom happening to you and you open your eyes to the gift, you realize that you do not own wis-dom. You are simply affected by wisdom. Unlike knowledge you can keep, wisdom is for you to give away. Giving wisdom is a dance of Tao, which propels the giving and receiving momentum. Once you live your Tao, you'll find a way to begin and sustain this miraculous dance. After thirty some years of teaching/learning, I call myself now a perpetual Dancestudent of the Tao .

9

A Teacher of Natural Spiritual Truth

Hua Ching Ni

As a young boy, Hua Ching Ni was taught the wisdom of the Way by his father, himself part of an unbroken lineage of Taoist teachers dating back many generations. He then studied with various teachers, recluses and hermits in the high mountains of China. Some years ago he came to this country to teach and write, founding Yo San Universtiy of Traditional Chinese Medicine and authoring a number of books on various aspects of the Taoist arts.

A warm and generous man, his unlined face at odds with his age (somewhere in his eighties), he laughs often and easily. At the same time, he speaks with the authority of experience and a wisdom gained though long years of study and practice.

He says about himself, "I was not especially gifted and encouraged. What I attained is through hard work and a challenging life. I have dedicated my life to support people who come though a hard life and grow through diligent learning. This is my personal offering to all my friends."

Do you feel that Taoism transcends cultural backgrounds?

I would say that the Western mind has more organization. It tends to make things nicely organized. In the Oriental mentality, we allow what is natural to continue to happen. If you go to a big American city, in the front yard of each house the grass has to be cut neatly, otherwise your neighbor will complain. You pay a price for their appreciation of what "should be done" and interfere with the yard's natural growth. In China, no one will say, "Why don't you cut your lawn in the front yard?"

This is not the main point. The main point is that the map of the two hemispheres of the human brain is similar to Eastern and Western thought. The mentalities are different. They help each other. One is good at organization and one is open to the natural truth. If there is too much organization it destroys the total natural reality, resulting in an unbeneficial situation. If you are too natural without any organization, then you become unruly and wild. If you have grass and let it grow naturally, it will grow too long and full of weeds. Both sides compliment and help one another with new direction and human hope.

So Taoism can come from China into this culture, and people can use it with their organizing abilities, yet it still frees us.

Right. You are too organized. You have organized religion, organized culture. Everything is organized, but you don't see the real things (laughter). In the Orient, they don't talk too much about how a gift is wrapped. They ask, "What is the meaning of the gift you are giving me?" It is not to say you have to buy some colorful paper to wrap it up nicely. That's not important. It's what your heart gives. What is meaningful is the gift itself. We should have the eyes to see the gift clearly, not how it is wrapped. The sincerity is the important thing. Often, the gift of the heart is expressed through the marketplace. You see many people shopping at Christmas time, taking lots of trouble to choose gifts. That is not real. They are living for the small things.

Taoism is not an ideology, not a religion, not something that you can join. So how can individuals get involved personally?

We first need to develop understanding. We believe that in the universe there is a subtle law, sometimes translated as "The Way." Look at anyone, including spirits and gods; if they live with this subtle law, then there is survival. They can prosper and there is abundance because it is allowed to happen. On the contrary, if you don't understand the subtle law, you create lots of human laws, which seem to bring only more trouble, not joy of life at all. If you live life too tightly, superficially, you are not living in the reality of the natural joy of life.

So many people seem to be so removed from the subtle universal law. They don't know how to even connect with it.

So this is a different way to develop one's self. First you work on your mentality. You develop your mentality to understand the substance of life. Development is not the furtherance of the preachers of any church. They are very good salesman. These people can sell anything. Unfortunately, some people see the belief in the words that fall from their mouths. They don't really look at it, they don't see through the dark to develop themselves, so they may experience it themselves and find the truth.

That is what I appreciate about Taoism: the emphasis on self-culti-vation, and not waiting for an intermediary, such as the priest, be-tween me and the Source. A lot of people don't want to take re-sponsibility for their own self-cultivation.

Right. That is the key point. So the first thing to ask is, "Am I willing to take my own responsibility"? If you are not, you will probably buy some ready-made program, as some people do. One should say, "I will now, at this moment, take responsibility for my own life. Then, I can reject or decide the value of the ready-made, conventional cul-tural system. The main thing is for me to develop more completely to understand how possible it is for these intermediaries to be of any real service to me and my opening.

Most people are taught by organized religion to give their responsi-bility up to the priest, rabbi, or something like that. People aren't taught in this culture to assume self responsiblity.

That is conventional religion. You can see that this type of teaching in most religions only creates obstacles for people's individual spiri-tual growth. You create more hostility between people if you believe in this way, because the belief is artificial. It is not the observed spiritual nature with which you are born. For example, observe a group of little children before they go to school or Sunday school. All children come along and play quite well. They don't look at what are their beliefs. Other people will ask that you consider what church they go to. Some religions are very aggressive and fight for their beliefs. Is there any meaning to this? In other words, it is less likely for this to occur if you are young at heart. If your heart is young, no matter how old you are, your mind is young. So wait for every spring. You are always opening up with totally new spirituality.

Like being flexible.

Right. In Taoism that is called being soft.

That's what drew me to Taoism. I started studying Chinese medicine. Then I asked what the philosophy was behind Chinese medicine. There's so much freedom in Taoism. To me it is total freedom and total self-responsibility.

In Western medicine, they first need to decide on a name for the disease before they can treat you. They ignore the interconnections and the wider context of the problem. This is only partial vison, because all diseases happen as a result of the process of your whole life, your life style.

You first need to correct your life. You don't need to examine the different ways that the culture is treating you, so that everything is established externally. Surely, I believe that internal and external are meeting each other. When these two are united you can help people observe other people better. Concentrating only on the externals will not really help. Solutions cannot come from only one side.

In spiritual work there is a principle. One is all. All is one. Each is one god. Totally, all the spirits are God. It is not separate at all. So it is beneficial to read my books to awaken your spiritual energy and to realize that we do not just have a main soul living in the body/house. The whole being is made of different levels of energy. *Qi* is physical energy. *Shen* is spiritual energy. Slowly, through your achievement, through your growth, all your spiritual agents become more effective in your work, and assist in creating the beauty of life. It comes naturally.

I have heard different things about reincarnation. Lao Tzu doesn't talk about it. Chuang Tzu doesn't talk about it. Some people have told me that it really a Buddhist idea, and that in the old days, Taoists believed that when you are dead, the hun and po separate, go into the earth and back out, and then there is no longer a personality.

That is only partial knowledge. Spirit is immortal, life can be renewed. The *hun* is not single. The *po* is not single. Reincarnation of a group of spirits involves the principle of spiritual evolution in which the healthier ones reincarnate

Not all of them?

Not all. If the whole group of spirits come together, the person will become organized again. It is only part of that person. As I described earlier, one is all, all is one. In each person's body, there are numerous spirits. Each one is exactly the same as the person is.

Each one exactly?

Exactly. For example, let's say someone dies. Through a channel or medium who has some real achievement, the spirits of the dead person can be invited to give a message to the family of the deceased. On such an occasion, perhaps the more active spirits will respond to the memories, the same affections from the words of the family. These active spirits still have the opportunity to be reborn, to live on, to perch on a new life. Reincarnation is not a law for all. For some it is a possibility; for some it is not a possibility. It is a very natural thing. But it is not as structured as Indian people teach. If someone dies, the personality is de-personalized. No main soul exists. Some spirits are like the discs of a computer with stored memory that can be retrieved into a new life. But a piece of memory by itself is of no value. It cannot be recreated unless it enters a new life.

So it is based on spiritual achievement or that kind of thing as to who gets reincarnated?

Life is the opportunity for you to further develop your spiritual life. If you cannot utilize the life opportunity, you have wasted it. This is why it is so important to spiritually develop oneself. For example, it is hard for you to agree with general, conventional religion because you have spent your lifetime learning and have achieved. At a certain time you know the force of the truth. You have devoted a lot of energy to seeing the truth directly, without the middleman salesmanship (of religion). You have already come to the stage to further your higher spiritual learning and spiritual development. I see that you have come to have different ideas about life.

I have often wondered about why there are so many people who are suffering. People in China and all over the world don't seem to ever get a chance to develop themselves. What is their life for or about? What happens to them?

In the human world, within your own family, or between husband and wife or different friends, the spiritual development in each person is vastly different. They say God is living in the world. They are also living in the world. They have human shapes but they are still beasts. (laughter). You cannot judge the people by their shape, you can judge by their internal spiritual shape.

Is that because of what they've done in a previous life?

No, they are made by their development. They do not come from the already trained and experienced development of the soul before, but they have just newly entered life from a different soul.

So what if these people never develop themselves?

They waste their life opportunity.

Then what happens to them?

It is a new integration, but this is an integration of the *hun* and *po* and everything that comes in from a lower level. Naturally, the *qi* is scattered.

So, it is not like you get another chance?

No. There are two levels. One achievement is to become a *hsien* or divine immortal. The other way is becoming a ghost. For example, when people die, the spirit beings of their life separate. The spirits can reorganize after this separation, so they pull the physical spirits to live with the skeleton under the ground. If anybody disturbs the grave, the phantom of the deceased spirits can sometimes show themselves unconsciously. If nobody intentionally disturbs the grave, sometimes there is a new building and something happens. You know when something happens because those spirits don't know how to be freely active. They only stay there until they are discovered. In general, once people die, their spirits scatter in the sky. There is no personality left.

Does this same principle apply with children who die in infancy?

No, in infancy they have a chance to come back. They have more of a chance because they don't have any life experience. They are pure. They will reach to the mother and father again. It is much easier. They have much more of a chance than the others who are out of their spiritual and physical energy. Everything is gone before they die. The others are like people who use up all their savings in the bank. They would simply become bigger debtors.

Now why is that? Why are some people more developed than others?

The universe is like this. Equality is not the truth. We are asking and wishing for equality. This is all a myth. You wish we are politically equal, spiritually equal. Basically, we stand equally, but how much you learn is different. How much you achieve is different. One person works hard and becomes rich. One person doesn't work and doesn't become rich. One person never has money and never knows the value of money because of mismanagment. He never conserves his life. One person earns a better living, knows the value of money, and conserves his life quite well. The same group of students attend the same school. How about achievement? There is a vast difference. They are building their interest in life.

These differences make life interesting. If everybody were the same the world would be very dull.

Some people believe everything happens for a reason. Everything happens because you create your own reality. Have you heard that phrase? You fall down the stairs and ask, "Why did I do that to myself? I have to figure out why I did that." And then there is the idea that sometimes things just happen.

There is a certain philosphy developed for people who say, "I fall down the stairs, ah...This is my fortune; this is my personal life karma. I can accept it." That helps them to cope, right? But the reality is that if you are walking down the street a tile will fly down to hit you. You should just think that this is natural. Why should I be mad about it? Right? If you are not developed, you say "Damn! What a bad day!" Your reaction is different. But, practically, there are lots of incidents with no purpose. They are natural accidents.

From what I understand, most young people today in China don't even know who Lao Tzu is. They don't know anything about the Tao Te Ching.

It is true.

Do you think it will come back?

Yes. If China becomes a free society, people will have a chance to be open to all kinds of life wisdom.

Do you think there is a chance that China will become a free society again?

China? It is necessary. In human history, darkness happens in certain states. Darkness can never stay forever. You can call this time a stage of darkness in Chinese culture. It will change and it will start to be a new time.

In your book, Harmony, the Art of Life, you write a lot about the harmony between the sexes. Couldn't that also be applied to harmony between races and different peoples? What is real harmony?

Your harmony is your development. If, in the same house, the wife and husband have similar understanding, no big problems develop. If the wife or husband have different levels of understanding or no power of understanding at all, they would not be able to live together in peace. This would not bring any happiness, only sickness and trouble.

Taoism is different in that there is nothing to join. You don't get to wear certain colors to label yourself. It is hard for people to understand.

I am ready to give as much freedom as is needed in order for new mentors to teach. You can organize groups differently, utilizing other ways for Western people to feel comfortable. You can set up a very good system to join. We have the *Universal Society of the Integral Way.* It is a non-committal way of joining, respecting the differences between people so they maintain their freedom. It is a very loose organization. People cultivate their own devotion, and year by year they grow. They enjoy this type of teaching. This is important to the Western mind. You need to think about how you organize the old teachings for a new society.

All the sages talk about the heavenly kingdom. The heavenly kingdom should be somewhere within the individual. It should be right here between yourself and your friends, whether they be in your study group or with whatever friends you reach. Because people trust you, there is no violence, no deceitfulness, only love and peace in helping each other. Then the teachings will be useful. If the heavenly kingdom is idealized as a place to be after death, it would be too far to reach. This is not practical. (laughter) I would like you to promote the heavenly kingdom right now, here in this world. In Buddhist terms, it is called the Pure Land. This is the same kind of concept as to realize the Messiah. Is it that you yourself intend to be a Messiah or are helping in the realization of the real Messiah? We cannot wait.

If you have true awareness of why you have come over here again, I mean why the soul has reincarnated, you must not only make a living but must also have an inner goal. If you are very clear, you offer selfless spiritual service. How long will it take for people to accept you as a spiritual teacher? It takes a long time to build the spiritual trust of people. Even if you are a very achieved soul and come back to the world, the world is a very different place than it was before.

From the last lifetime?

Yes, it is different than your last life when it was simple. You think you can manage it once you come over here, but you cannot.

In this new society, during the past forty or fifty years of what you call the new age, many teachers have arisen, some of whom are very famous. They have lots of money and respect, but did they do anything for the world? They may have only expressed themselves negatively with their own example. Many teachers do that. Many teachers only work to build themselves.

However, we are not going to play the same trick as the teachers of other generations, making people who are religious followers become Christian, Islamic, Buddhist, or even Taoist. We give selfless spiritual service and only want to help people achieve a deeper understanding, and have better health in all aspects of their lives. They become people of depth for their own purpose, as well as people of spiritual impartiality. We help people become good people.

My goal is very simple. It is to have a better world with better people. It's not about teaching people to serve my ego, like a spiritual ruler. This is a new approach. Only a person who has freedom from financial and other worldly pressure can do this kind of spiritual work of uplifting the world spiritual condition. I can afford to do that. Other teachers cannot because they are struggling for emotional aggrandizement and financial survival.

Isn't there a tradition of your family to work as doctors and do the spiritual work on the side?

Self-support is the foundation of pure spiritual service. When I was young and my interests were very broad, my father showed me by example that I needed to become a Chinese doctor. I needed to earn my own bread in order to really pass the truth to other people. If you are concerned with how many people you can get to come to you because you need income, then what are you doing? You always need to please people who come to hear the truth.

The deeper truth is very simple. All human experience can see that no particular religion is greater than another. The universal spiritual essence of each individual has a general religious spirit. I call that natural piety, that is a kind of pure devotion to all life. That is the best kind of universal religious spirit of impartiality.

Just like shooting an arrow to a target, many religions and religious teachers either go too much to the left or too much to the right, too high or too low, and miss the center of the target. Most religions miss it, because only a few go directly to the center. If you never do express this piety toward any valuable thing, you also miss it. The most important thing is the broad universal spiritual piety, not toward any specific expression, but toward your own pure essence of life and the good life of all others.

I call this natural piety the Universal Divine One. It is God itself. You don't need to go back 2000 years to have a divine being talk to you. The true spiritual teachers make people better for the sake of the people themselves, and they make a better world for the sake of the world. They don't make people better for their control and for one partial religion.

Do you think that a strong soul who has accomplished a lot in previous lives can come back to this life and remember or reconstruct their previous accomplishments for this life or does one have to start from scratch every time? Do you bring with you the achievements you've attained in the past?

There are two ways. Some really achieved souls may be able to keep all their achievement. For example, when you put your foot into the river, and then take it out and put it in again, it's new water. You came back to learn over again. Most spiritual teachers have past life experiences and some of them drown in the current by forgetting the inner goal. Usually if a divine being comes back again, he already knows the taste of life. He has no reason to come back to swim in the bitter salt water again, but he may have made a vow or subtle wish to come back to help the world.

Some people seem to be naturally more interested in spiritual matters than others, or are more spiritually directed. Is that because they have done spiritual work before and so when they come back to this lifetime, they are drawn to the spiritual work?

There are all kinds of cases. Your life experiences are very important. If you feel that a certain part of your life is unfulfilled, you will have a certain attachment to it, and that is the reason you come back. For instance, if you are a man and see a woman for whom there is a natural attraction, you may come back because that line of desire was not fulfilled. You come back just to be married.

Another instance is, if you are in a Buddhist monastery and practice Zen Buddhism, you have been enlightened that a natural life is a good model of life. However, living in a monastery is not an excellent model of life. It may be good for your personal spiritual cultivation, but it is not a good model of life, and since you don't have skills for a social life, you need to come back again to live correctly. You already understand all the enlightenment that you have reached in your last life, but you need to come back for the social part.

You're saying that if someone was living in a monastery who didn't fulfill the worldly life and didn't do their cultivation in the world, that they would have to come back again so that they could do it in the world this time?

If you have achievement, you have enlightenment and you will be able to discover your mistake, so you will fulfill it directly. Do not postpone the important enlightenment. Thinking is the seed of being. When you're young, if you think about stealing, later you may become a thief. I repeat, thinking is the seed of being. So in general, if you come back to a new life, you still have the seeds from the last life. So, the past life, present life and future can all be seen just in the short span of this lifetime.

But, as you said earlier, not everyone reincarnates.

Even when they reincarnate they don't know they were here, because they may live with low self-consciousness. So sometimes they may have spiritual achievement in this new opportunity but it doesn't equal the achievement of the previous life. In other words, somebody may live on the edge of the wheel of the life, but if their achievement enables them to comes close to the hub of the wheel, there are fewer or no changes in their life. The wheel of the world turns around, but you don't turn with it, you keep your center.

Some people may feel that they don't have to work to achieve anything in this life, but they think, 'I'll just do it next lifetime.' Some people think that they'll just be born over and over again until they come to some understanding.

You can only help people who are really troubled by life. Those individuals struggle in their life to collect themselves. Teaching something very exotic will always be very popular, but it hardly brings people to the Way.

I always put people back to a normal worldly life to cure them, to help them. It is very hard work. You need to assist them, because they don't like life in the world. They want deliverance and salvation away from the world. They don't like to be cured by being restored to their normal track of life.

Sometimes I ask myself why I don't teach Zen Buddhism or esoteric Buddhism or some other cultural style. Year after year, I just guide people back to their good life. It's the most difficult thing to do; it's really challenging.

Now I am working to restore the world as a good world, as a happy world. This cannot be accomplished by one individual. I need lots of help, lots of good individuals to come together. I don't require people to become a Taoist, I don't require them to serve me for my own benefit. We are working to have a better world with better people. No matter what your religious preference, you can do this work. I am not concerned about your religious background. I guide people who wish to open up and learn the spiritual learning from their own growth and maturity.

Do you feel that the human race has a limited amount of time to make this transition, or do you feel like that its already been accomplished from the bigger picture of eternity? Do you feel that we have to start waking up or do you feel that time will take us there, without us having to worry too much about it?

I can answer this question in two ways. One way is that the ones who came here to fulfill their purpose of helping the world know that spiritual work has no measurement of big or small. It is not a circus, like the religious priests who have to put on special costumes and have lots of attendants and make a big show. That is not real life. We talk about real life. Those who have achieved themselves are not looking for more achievement for themselves, but for the world.

Your question is about how much time we have. It seems that the time runs short. In ancient times, people had already developed a way to look at the stars and how their formation could have such an affect on such a small world. We sometimes make the world so big, but the world is really very small. Anything can affect us. If you don't believe that, consider a comet shooting into the earth. If it really hit hard, what would happen? Anything can happen. So the time to awaken is now.

This world is still small, very small. Each person needs their own spiritual awareness to look at the signs in the coming years, and each of us needs to prepare for it.

Conventional religions talk about God, and say that God has chosen the priests to act as the middle person between people and God. This type of joke cannot continue to work. My teaching is different. We already see the signs, so why not respect the sky? Why don't the people themselves change the trouble before the trouble happens? This is a minimum self rescue. The rescue happens by awakening to one's own soul. I offer the guidance through my various publications.

Some spiritual teachers say that the earth is so polluted and the politi-

cal climate is so bad that we will destroy ourselves. Other people think that a golden age will come and everyone will be spiritual.

I don't think that either will happen. In order for the world to survive after the year 2000, we must change ourselves constructively. We must stop fooling ourselves.

So you don't feel that we are heading for destruction nor that we have to really worry about it?

My approach is different. In ancient times, when there was an eclipse people would panic. The wise one would look at it and look to himself to see if he had some sort of shortcoming in life or behavior. He would then make a change. Whenever there is some sort of destruction on earth, we all need to see that as a sign of a spiritual warning for us to do better in our lives.

Many people use the doomsday doctrine to make people scared. I would instead look at the potential for natural calamity or any astrological event as an opportunity to reflect and make some changes.

The universe is all connected as one by what I call natural conscious energy. The earth is alive, and all the stars are alive. This conscious energy can be used to communicate with and understand one another. I also call it the universal mind. If we change our mind, then our fortune can change, too.

Sometimes when people try to take the essence of all religions, they just end up watering it all down.

It's true. This is why religions are not the direct truth. A religion is one way of communicating.

When I was in Los Angles, where I spent more time around people, individuals of all kinds of religious backgrounds enjoyed my books. I often found out what their spiritual background was. If they were Christian, I told them to pray to God, and if they were Buddhist, I told them to pray to Buddha. This is a way of communicating. The real Buddha or real God is a natural untitled spiritual being of great life. All religion is only a type of spiritual language.

*Like what they used to say about the finger pointing to the moon,
'don't look at the finger, look at the moon.'*

The water may show you a reflection of the moon, but that is not the
real moon. It is only a reflection. The moon is still far away in the sky.

*So these days you are challenging your students to go beyond even
Taoism and reach the very essence of spiritual truth.*

Right. You must always look at the truth behind and between the
lines. Don't become stuck by any terminology.

*Does the highest level of spiritual achievement connect one with
the source of all life?*

You can be very small, and you can also be very big to include the
universe. I myself enjoy living in a big multi-dimensional world rather
than a small world like the earth. The United States and China are
both parts of the small world. It takes many years to make it possible
for a few astronauts to travel to the moon, but with spiritual development you can fly anywhere you want. Your body is your house, and
you can go outside of the house by riding on the light.

Once you become achieved, however, you see that there is no
difference between life and death, and no difference between staying here or going somewhere else. At that time, you can witness God
and all the achieved ones. They maybe in human form, or they may
not be.

Not many people achieve that level.

It is very hard. You need special training, concentration, and experience. The growth is attained step by step.

*What do we do today as students who want to achieve when so
much of the tradition has been lost?*

It depends on the new spiritual effort on the old spiritual root. People can read my books for the confirmation of their own attainment.

In one of your books you talked about how people can connect with spiritual teachers who are spirit helpers.

That is one level. It depends upon the individual's own spiritual foundation. When you are able to do that, you will also have certain experiences of the poly-dimensional life and the proof of the existence of other levels of life.

However, each individual's inspiration is different. I may teach one thing, but each individual may understand it differently. Their benefit is also different. This is the interesting part of the human world.

We can only do our best. Human power is still limited. We need to work together to improve the world. Even if we don't have the force, we still have the power, which is based on the law of correspondence, the natural energy correspondence. This power for change will affect everything. Spiritual power does make the world change, although it is very subtle. Don't wait passively, saying that the world will change by itself. Don't let doomsday come to your life or to the world. Change the doomsday into a brighter day.

Your spiritual practice, your spiritual viewpoint and your positive spiritual influence will help. Don't worry about it. This is what we can do. Physically we are limited, but spiritually we are not limited. We need to change ourselves first and the world will follow.

The Abode of the Eternal Tao

The Empty Vessel, A Journal of Contemporary Taoism.
A quarterly publication dedicated to the exploration and dissemination of nonreligious Taoist philosophy and practice. Learn practical applications of Taoist thought, *tai ji*, internal arts, Chinese medicine and *qi gong*. Enjoy articles, interviews and feature stories that show how contemporary practitioners have incorporated a balance of body, mind and spirit into their lives.
Includes art, poetry, essays and reviews of the latest books, tapes and videos. *The Empty Vessel* is the only journal of its kind, covering all aspects of Taoist philosophy and practice in a thought-provoking and timely manner.
Subscriptions are $18 per year. Sample issue $6.50 postpaid.

Traditions of Tao Chinese Herbal Formulas
These food-grade formulas are a comprehensive nutritional foundation. Viewed as a food supplement, the action and nature of the formulas are cleansing, nourishing, strengthening, balancing and energizing. For a free catalogue of Traditions of Tao formulas write or call The Abode of the Eternal Tao.

Qi Gong.
The Abode of the Eternal Tao has certified instructors in several forms of *qi gong* and Taoist meditation. To inquire about a class or workshop in your area call or write.

The Abode of the Eternal Tao
4852 West Amazon
Eugene, OR 97405
Or call 1-800-574-5118 for credit card orders.